The immediate p[...] [...] of this book is to undertake a systematic investigation of the extent to which the question of unity dominated Teilhard de Chardin's thought as well as his spirituality. The ultimate purpose is that this investigation of a notion central to Teilhard's work should lead to a more intelligent and fruitful reading of his writings.

Attention is focused primarily upon Teilhard's early period, roughly 1916-1927, the period climaxed by the writing of *Le Milieu Divin*. The importance of this apparent limitation of attention lies in the fact that this is a period vital to Teilhard's development and yet one that has not yet received the study that is necessary if the reader of Teilhard is to develop a more precise understanding of his total *corpus*.

The author's starting point is what he describes as Teilhard's "theory of creative union", which he presents as the key to an understanding of the whole of Teilhard's thought. The author shows in very clearly argued steps how Teilhard's theory that creation proceeds through the unification of multiplicity permeates his view of reality. The content of this theory is established in the opening chapter and what follows thereafter is an elucidation of the theory in relation to the total progression of Teilhard's ideas, expanding into an excellent and original expository study of Teilhard's thought.

This lucidly written book, which combines sensitive criticism with much original research, is bound to be of service to all those anxious to unravel Teilhard's key notions, and to familiarize themselves with the driving impulse that characterized his early period of work and that later came to fruition.

Univers[...]as
BIBLIOTHECA
Ottaviensis

The One and the Many

The One and the Many

Teilhard de Chardin's Vision of Unity

Donald P. Gray

London · Burns & Oates

Universitas
BIBLIOTHECA
Ottaviensis

BURNS & OATES LIMITED
25 Ashley Place, London S.W.1

First published 1969

B
2430
.T374G68
1969

© 1969 by Herder and Herder Inc.

SBN: 223 97765 9

Made and printed in Great Britain by
William Clowes and Sons, Limited, London and Beccles

Contents

To Maureen, who made it possible,
and John, David, and Ellen,
who at times tried to make it impossible.

The One and the Many

Preface

This book came into being as the child of a somewhat unusual, in part original, reading of the writings of Teilhard de Chardin. That Teilhard aspired after unity is well enough recognized on all sides. However, no one, so far as I know, has attempted to investigate systematically to what extent the whole question of unity or union dominates Teilhard's thought as well as his spirituality. The purpose of this volume is to do precisely that in the hope that it will lead to a more intelligent and fruitful reading of Teilhard himself. This is a volume not only *about* Teilhard but *for* him as well.

What is perhaps most unusual about the approach adopted here, quite apart from the overarching perspective chosen, is the fact that a preponderance of attention has been devoted to Teilhard's early period, that is the period from roughly 1916 to 1927, the period climaxed by the writing of *The Divine Milieu*. This is not a stage of Teilhard's development which is particularly well appreciated in the United States at the present time. What I hope to have shown in these pages is that this period is quite crucial for the accurate interpretation of Teilhard's total corpus of writings. During these years Teilhard was much more explicitly engaged in the elucidation of philosophical and theological themes than in most of his later writings. That Teilhard's concerns were abidingly religious from start to finish becomes abundantly clear from a study of the early period.

Since the purpose of a preface is presumably to clarify as much as possible the reading adventure about to follow, it might be well at this juncture to say something about the history of this book and then to define more exactly the task which I have set myself.

Like many another scholarly publication today, these pages were initially worked out as a doctoral dissertation. What impressed me most during my first extensive reading of Teilhard's writings was what might be termed in English his theory of creative union. What is meant by this expression is explained in detail in Chapter I. For me personally, it gradually became the key to understanding the whole of Teilhard's thought, even though for most commentators it occupies at best a marginal importance in their exegesis of Teilhard's work.

Admittedly, the theory of creative union does not bulk large in Teilhard's actual writings. However, the penetrating and basically simple insight capsulized in this theory, namely that creation proceeds through the unification of multiplicity, structures and permeates Teilhard's view of reality. The original study focused very heavily on the theory of creative union as the key to understanding Teilhard's thought and spirituality. The same is still largely true of the present book which represents an abridgement and partial rewriting of that original statement.

What perhaps needs to be stressed is a point which I only lately came to appreciate myself. What has guided my own reading of Teilhard more than the theory of creative union as such or the explicit references to it, is the basic insight which is contained in it and which was alluded to above. Fixing on that insight, I have proceeded to relate everything else of importance in Teilhard's writings to it and in this way have attempted to achieve a synthesis of his thought. The synthesis as it stands here in these pages was never worked out in quite this way by Teilhard himself. Themes are brought into interrelationship here which Teilhard seems never to have interconnected in quite this fashion. Is the synthesis Teilhardian? The reader will have to make up his own mind about that. All that can be said in defense of this procedure is that it introduces considerable coherence into the totality of Teilhard's thought and serves to illuminate it in a rather striking way.

It would undoubtedly be somewhat presumptuous for a commentator to claim that he has gone to the heart of another man's vision, laid bare his fundamental insight into reality, and subsequently restructured his thought in a way which is at points clearer and tighter than the original synthesis. With due restraint, then, let it only be said that the approach adopted here has proved to be a personally helpful point of entry into a great man's mind and spirit and that it is offered to a broader public only in the hope that others will find in these pages a way of reading Teilhard that will prove equally instructive and fruitful. This study is not primarily intended as a critical study, even though some few criticisms of Teilhard are offered. Rather, it is offered as an expository study of and introduction to Teilhard's thought and spirituality. The only justification for adding another entry to the seemingly endless Teilhard bibliography is that this book is not quite like any other study of Teilhard presently available, although it covers the same ground in some cases. Nor is it simply the condensed sum total of other works already available. It purports at least to provide "a somewhat unusual, in part original, reading of the writings of Teilhard de Chardin," drawn primarily from a dialogue with Teilhard's own thought and only subsidiarily from secondary sources.

Having set out the general import of what it is to follow, we may now briefly indicate something of the details of the procedure used to present Teilhard's vision of unity. In Chapter I it is argued that the problem of the one and the many lies at the heart of Teilhard's questioning, and that the theory of creative union constitutes his response to this problem. Having thus dealt with the notion of creation through union in a general way, succeeding chapters work out the specifics of the movement of creation in terms of the relationship between matter and spirit (Chapter II) and between the person and the community (Chapter IV). The problem of evil as threat to unity is worked through in Chapter III, while the interaction and interdependence of the One God and the pluralistic creation is discussed in Chapters V and VI. Chapter VII takes up the various threads of Teilhardian spirituality in an attempt to show how they are related to his vision of unity and how they in fact flow quite naturally out of it. Finally, the concluding summary essays to restate the broad lines of the argument.

The study from which this book has been hewn was written in the Theology Department at Fordham University. Its point of view is decidedly theological even though it incorporates a good deal of material which is not *ex professo* theological in keeping with the nature of the subject of this study. Teilhard may not have been a theologian, although it is not totally clear why he may not be considered one depending on one's definition of terms, but he certainly must be styled a religious thinker. His work arises out of religious concerns, both personal and apologetic, and is religious in intent. The theory of creative union, as will be made clear later, is a theological perspective even if it proves to be fruitful outside the theological circle as well.

No work of scholarship, however modest in character, could ever see the light of day apart from a supporting and encouraging environment, and in this particular case the environment was especially congenial. I must first of all thank Father Christopher Mooney, S.J., who not only planted the seeds but watered them as well and brought them to fruition. Secondly, I should like to thank Dr. Ewert Cousins and Father Joseph Donceel, S.J., who served as readers and made many helpful suggestions for improving the text. In the third place, I should like to express my appreciation to Mr. Justus George Lawler of Herder and Herder whose interest from the very beginning and throughout is alone responsible for the present publication. A word of appreciation is also due to The Danforth Foundation whose generosity made possible a two year leave of absence from Manhattan College which resulted in the completion of this study. And finally, I should like to express publicly my gratitude to my wife, who typed the manuscript at all the varied stages of its development, but whose contribution goes far beyond that, as any author-husband knows.

I

Creative Union

The Problem of the One and the Many

"Science, philosophy, and religion alike have all been basically concerned with the resolution of but one single problem: that of the relationship between multiplicity and unity."[1] It is to the resolution of this single problem that the thought of Pierre Teilhard de Chardin is itself devoted. Such at least is the argument of the following pages.

The problem of the one and the many is a comprehensive problem, the stuff of which systems are made. It is a problem which poses a question for both thought and action. The unification of the multiple in synthetic thought can only be a preliminary step towards a unification of the multiple in synthetic action. Either human thought and human activity must rest content with the obvious fragmented pluralism of the given world of experience, or human thought and human activity must seek, in one way or another, to go beyond pluralism in the direction of unity.

Is the One alone real and the multiple merely illusion? Is the multiple alone real so that the world is irremediably and irreducibly pluralistic at its core? Is the world a gigantic process consisting in the unification of a multiplicity destined to be brought into a higher unity with the One? These are questions which have always fascinated the speculative mind, and they are the questions which fascinated Teilhard de Chardin, a man with a speculative cast of mind of extraordinary brilliance. Teilhard essayed in his writings a solution to the overarching and ancient problem of the one and the many, but from a new perspective, that of evolution. Such would seem to be the fate of every significant thinker: to wrestle with the perennial problems of human existence, but from an original point of view which gives rise to a new synthesis.

In actuality the problem of the one and the many constitutes a threefold problem for Teilhard. First of all, the problem of the one and the many is a problem of the relationship between matter and spirit. Secondly, it is a problem of the relationship between the individual and the total community of humanity. And finally, it is a problem of the relationship between the one God and the pluralistic world of creatures which he has brought into being, although, in a very real sense, the problem of the one and the many is initially for Teilhard a problem of the inner trinitarian life of God as well. In the first part of this first chapter we will be concerned with the problem of the one and the many as it relates to the process of trinitization within the divine life itself and subsequently as it relates to the act of creation *ex nihilo*. In the second part of the chapter, we will try to set out the main lines of Teilhard's theory of creative union, the theory which lies at the heart of Teilhard's attempted solution to the problem of the one and the many.

The Process of Trinitization

The thought of Teilhard is unmistakably christocentric throughout —so much so that it might well appear that he is in reality a christomonist who allows little if any place in his system for the doctrine of the Trinity. While Teilhard does not speak frequently of the trinitarian doctrine, he does not by any means simply ignore it. It is not, however, until we reach 1948 that we find Teilhard's most developed statement on the trinitarian doctrine as it relates to the problem of the one and the many and more specifically to the question of creation. Seeking to work out the various moments or stages of his metaphysics of union, he comments thusly on the significance and sense of the trinitarian doctrine:

It is absolutely necessary to begin, in the first moment of our dialectic, by presupposing as simply given (and at this point we in no way diverge from the procedure of classical philosophy) the existence of an irreversible and self-sufficient "Supreme Being" (what we ourselves have termed Point Omega). Without making such a presupposition, it would be quite impossible (logically as well as ontologically) to make sense of anything, that is to say it would be quite impossible to go any further in our analysis. However, if such a Center, both the origin and goal of everything else, is to be able to subsist in itself in total independence of everything else, it must be further assumed (in conformity with the data of revelation—and here we find ourselves at the second moment of our dialectic) that this Center is constituted by internal trinitarian relations. In this way, the ontological principle upon which our metaphysics is based is seen to hold good even at the most profound and indeed primordial level of being: God himself, in a rigorously real sense, only exists through a process of self-unification.[2]

The trinitarian formulation thus provides the key to understanding the whole movement of reality as a process of unification. Teilhard has in this way discovered the significance for his own system of thought of the quite traditional idea that the Trinity is the archetype of creation. In order to appreciate all the ramifications of this archetype-image dialectic, we must follow Teilhard in the development of the remaining moments of his metaphysics of union as these relate to the problem of creation.

Creation *ex nihilo*

In a text which appears to destroy the gratuity of creation, Teilhard sets out the third moment of his dialectic:

We have just seen that God trinitizes his own life in the very act of being himself. However, this is by no means the end of the matter. For by the very fact that the Supreme Being exists through a process of self-unification, he necessarily sets up another type of opposition, not at the heart of his own life, but rather at the farthest remove from it (we are now at the third moment of our dialectic). On the one hand, we have self-subsistent unity at the pole of being, and, on the other, all along the periphery of being, we are of necessity confronted with multiplicity. However, let it be made clear at the outset that we have in mind here a pure multiplicity or creatable nothingness, which is still nonetheless nothing, but which is a possibility (or plea) for being, owing to its passive virtuality for arrangement or union. In conclusion, we may add that the passage from the possibility of creation to its actualization occurs in such a way that it appears to us as if God could not resist the plea of multiplicity for concrete being. Obviously, in attempting to understand such a mysterious event the human mind is no longer able to distinguish clearly between absolute necessity and absolute freedom.[3]

What perhaps needs most to be stressed in relation to this text is that pure multiplicity functions for Teilhard simply as a category of thought, a limit-concept, derived dialectically from the category of unity or trinity. While the categories of pure multiplicity and non-being are in fact equivalent, the former is much harder to deal with because of the spontaneous tendency to imagine, and hence implicitly reify, pure multiplicity. The category of pure multiplicity in this way appears to threaten the Christian doctrine of creation *ex nihilo*, although this was not at all Teilhard's intention. Teilhard's language is admittedly somewhat overly picturesque and anthropomorphic, but important concerns lie behind his efforts here to articulate his thought.

All that we wish to emphasize for our purposes is that Teilhard thought, almost instinctively, in terms of unity and multiplicity rather than in terms of being and non-being. The trinitarian formulation is therefore found to be of considerable help in his attempts to understand the relationship between divine Being and created, or what he habitually calls "participated," being. God is to be understood as the divine Union, creatures by contrast are to be understood as a multiplicity undergoing union. If such is the case, then, "before creation," so to speak, we can only conceive of a sheer multiplicity—God is both one and in some sense diverse, the creatures apart from the One and his creative action would be simply diverse, multiple, or non-existent. If Teilhard's approach has its problems, it also incorporates some penetrating insights.

We are here at the deepest roots of Teilhard's system, for we are asking ourselves which categories are to be considered determinative of our understanding of reality. Teilhard's reply is unhesitating: unity and multiplicity. Being and non-being are to be considered subordinate to these without detriment, however, to the notion of creation *ex nihilo*.

Even if it is granted that Teilhard can be located tolerably within the bounds of traditional orthodoxy on this score, can his understanding of the gratuity of creation also be allowed the same toleration? Again, Teilhard had no intention of simply eliminating the traditional insistence on gratuity. However, he does wish to qualify it in such a way that it will not be construed as implying that the creation is a matter of indifference to God. This concern emerges very clearly in the fourth moment of the dialectic:

Classical philosophy (or theology) has invariably tended to represent creation or participation (the fourth moment of our dialectic) as an almost arbitrary gesture on the part of the First Cause. Creation, in such a view, is understood on the analogy of efficient causality and appears to be a totally arbitrary act, indeed "an act of God" in the pejorative sense of that phrase. According to a metaphysics of union, on the other hand, while the self-sufficiency and self-determination of the Supreme Being still remain intact (since, I must repeat again, the pure multiplicity at the antipodes of God is nothing more than pure potentiality and passivity), the creative act takes on a quite well-defined significance and structure. Creation is now seen to be, in some sense, a reflection of God outside of himself rather than within himself. Creation, or what St. Paul would have termed pleromization (that is the full actualization of participated being through arrangement and totalization) now appears to be a kind of symmetrical reduplication of trinitization. Creation, as it were, fills a void, it finds its proper place. And, at the same time, it becomes possible to speak of creation in the same terms that we have used to define being. To create is to unite.[4]

Creation is now seen to be no longer simply a fact accepted in faith, but rather a datum of faith which has intelligible meaning and motivating power for activity. "Creation, as it were, fills a void, it finds its proper place." It is no longer "a totally arbitrary act, indeed 'an act of God' in the pejorative sense of that phrase." Confronted with the possibility of unifying a pure multiplicity and bringing it finally to unity with himself, "it appears as if God could not resist the plea of multiplicity for concrete being." Is God forced into creating? "Obviously, in attempting to understand such a mysterious event the human mind is no longer able to distinguish clearly between absolute necessity and absolute freedom." Teilhard does not wish to say that creation is necessary if that is taken to mean that God is forced into acting from outside of himself; nor, however, does he want to say that creation is simply contingent if that is taken to mean that creation is a matter of mere indifference to God. Teilhard recognizes "in the infallible sign of love the presence of freedom"[5] in the creative act, but he does not want God's freedom to be understood as a *potentia absoluta* which acts without any discernible motivation.

What Teilhard finally discerns is not so much a necessity to creation as a pattern in creation. The movement of creation is an image of the movement of the divine life itself. The suggestion still remains, however, that something other than the love of God must be found to guarantee the seriousness of creation for God. Teilhard wants above all else to be assured that God is really committed to the work of the world's progress, that it really matters to him, that it makes a difference. If love is confused with sentimentality or whim, then the danger of an arbitrary act of creation becomes real indeed. Teilhard seems unable to arrive at an adequate understanding of God's love as the motive of creation because he has a confused notion of God's freedom, or rather he is constantly struggling against a faulty nominalistic understanding of God's freedom as a *potentia absoluta*. As a result, he keeps trying to unearth a more intelligible rationale to God's creative activity because of a fear that love is something irrational and leads in the end to arbitrary activity. The pattern which Teilhard rightly observes in creation is not a motive for creating but rather an expression of God's love for the world he creates. The gratuity of creation is not to be understood in the sense of a gratuitous remark, but rather in the sense of a gracious word of love. Teilhard is not attempting to destroy the gratuity of creation, but rather to get beyond a faulty understanding of it. Unfortunately, his own efforts at understanding fall short of the mark as well, but are, nonetheless, pointed in the right direction.

When all is said and done, however, Teilhard only intended his approach to be understood as a provisional attempt at theological understanding. He states this quite emphatically himself:

I naturally harbor no illusions with regard to the precarious and provisional character of such a metaphysic. Nonetheless I am also convinced that it is only by means of such efforts at understanding, moving as they do closer and closer to the truth by way of repeated approximations, that the universe gradually becomes coherent for our thought.... Such a tentative method of approximation holds just as good for philosophical reflection as it does for scientific investigation.[6]

If Teilhard is not able to come up with a completely satisfactory statement of the gratuity of creation, the fact remains that he does manage to obtain an insight into the relationship between the doctrines of the Trinity and creation.

By way of summary, we may say that for Teilhard the life of God is a dynamic process of trinitization and hence in some carefully qualified sense[7] the life of God appears to us in its root meaning as a victory of unity over multiplicity. The "many" are one in God without losing their differentiating characteristics. However, the trinitarian life of God is not an isolated life, closed in on its own dialectical movement, unrelated to the world of our own experience. Rather, the trinitarian life of God is the archetypal form of all life, of all reality. For Teilhard the whole of reality is a process involving the unification of the multiple, and this process in its entirety springs from God, is patterned upon his own life, and is destined to participate in that trinitarian life from which it has come.[8]

Pure Multiplicity in the Early Essays

While the dialectic of trinitization and creation achieved its most mature formulation only in 1948, Teilhard had wrestled with the problem as early as 1917:

In the beginning, then, there were, at the two poles of being, God and multiplicity. And yet God was quite alone inasmuch as multiplicity, because of its totally dissociated condition, did not in fact exist. From all eternity, God saw, at his feet, the fragmented shadow of his own unity. This shadow, while it possessed the capacity to become something, is not to be conceived of as another god because, of itself, it was nothing and never had been anything. Nor would it ever have been able to become anything since its very nature was to be infinitely divided in itself, that is to say, to exist in the realm of non-being. Infinitely vast and infinitely rarefied, the multiple, equivalent to non-being, was sound asleep at the antipodes of Being, Itself One and concentrated within Itself.

It was then that the One, overflowing with life, joined battle, through creation, with this non-existent multiplicity which stood in opposition to the One by way of defiant contradiction. *To create is, according to all appearances*, to condense, to concentrate, to organize, *to unify*.[9]

While the trinitarian doctrine lies behind this text by implication at least, it is never explicitly mentioned. Furthermore, the movement of the argument is somewhat more dramatic in form in that Teilhard pictures God as entering into a struggle with pre-creational multiplicity as if it were some thing which actually opposed him. However, it is perfectly plain that Teilhard wishes to remain within the context of a creation *ex nihilo* and decidedly does not intend to suggest that God has to struggle with a pre-existent chaos outside of himself. Although the language is admittedly faulty and the role of the imagination rather too predominant, the intent of the passage is evident enough.

In an essay written later the same year, Teilhard made a further attempt to give expression to the doctrine of creation but from the rather unilateral point of view of positive non-being. There can be little doubt that this particular statement of his position is unduly ambiguous and misleading. Having attempted to define, rather unsuccessfully, what he means by positive non-being, Teilhard acknowledges the difficulties inherent in his position:

I have no illusions about the fact that such a conception of a sort of positive non-being, which is the subject of creation, raises some serious problems. However deeply mired in non-being one supposes the initial multiplicity required for the action of creative union to have been, there still remains a suggestion that the Creator found, outside of himself, a support or at least some kind of reaction. Such a theory further suggests that creation was not absolutely gratuitous, but rather represents a work of almost absolute interest to God. Such a view obviously smacks of Manichaeism.

It is difficult to resolve such problems. However, is there really any way of avoiding such pitfalls (or rather such paradoxes) without resorting to merely verbal explanations? [10]

During the spring of the following year, Teilhard admits quite frankly that he has not yet been able to work out a doctrine of the pre-creational state to his own satisfaction: "I readily acknowledge that the theory of creative union, if not in its main thrust (which is close to Christ), at least *in its extension* to the initial creation and to the formation of the soul, stands in need of revision." [11]

Six years later, the question of a pre-creational multiplicity is taken up once again, but this time with an interesting change of perspective:

At the outermost limit of reality, impossible for us to imagine, we find an immense plurality—complete diversity joined to total disunity. The truth of the matter is that such an absolute multiplicity would be equivalent in fact to non-being, and it has of course never at any time existed as such. Rather, it is the direction from which the world emerges, at least as far as we are able to tell. At the beginning of time, the world reveals itself to us as coming forth from multiplicity and then as existing in a state of extreme multiplicity.[12]

The dialectical contrast between the One God and pure multiplicity is notably absent from this text. Teilhard is no longer proceeding by way of deduction from the One to its dialectical opposite pure multiplicity. Rather, the method is now inductive in character, proceeding backwards from the presently observed state of reality as a unified multiplicity to increasingly disunified and pluralistic states of reality. Teilhard is saying in effect that if one takes the actually existing world apart through analysis, one will be driven ever further backwards until one reaches a pure multiplicity which is equivalent to non-being and hence functions as a limiting concept to analysis rather than as the definition of an actually existing state of extreme plurality. No amount of scientific investigation will ever turn up pure multiplicity as such, for it is nothing and has existence only as a logical postulate. Again we see that if the human mind begins from an understanding of reality as unity rather than as being, it arrives inevitably at its polar opposite which is multiplicity. However, the two notions are actually identical.

We have already noted Teilhard's own uneasiness with the notion of pure multiplicity. However, the fact that he returned to it again as late as 1948 indicates that he could find no other way of expressing the matter that was compatible with his overall system. Teilhard was trying over the years to purify the notion of various objectionable elements which might tend to suggest that pure multiplicity was a pre-existing something which God unifies but does not bring into existence. His formulations of the concept after the First World War are quite circumspect and appear indeed to possess a certain validity within the context of a system basically concerned with the problem of unity and multiplicity and their interrelationship.

We are now in a position to summarize the results of our inquiry into the relationship between unity and multiplicity with respect to the pre-creational state. Preceding the act of creation itself, Teilhard postulates a pure multiplicity which he arrives at both deductively from the point of view of trinitization and inductively from the point of view of evolution as a process of unification. Teilhard habitually equates this pure multiplicity with non-being in order to safeguard the traditional Christian doctrine of creation *ex nihilo*. We have argued that for Teilhard pure multiplicity is a logical postulate, a limiting concept which expresses the polar opposite of perfect unity (the Trinity) as well as the final logical result of a method of analysis which seeks to divide reality retrogressively into increasingly pluralistic elements. It must be remembered that pure multiplicity is *not* a datum of experience or scientific investigation, but rather an abstraction from experience. We have further tried to argue that the concept of pure multiplicity has a certain symbolic validity in that it underlines the trinitarian structure of the divine life as a life of supreme unity and also in that it seeks to give shape to the movement of reality as a process involving the unification of the multiple.

Commentators have by no means been unanimous in their assessment of Teilhard's attempt to hypothesize about the pre-creational state in terms of pure multiplicity. One line of interpretation prefers to see in Teilhard's efforts a reincarnation of the ancient idea of a primeval struggle between God and a pre-existent chaos. This view stems principally from Claude Tresmontant:

The idea of a "struggle" between the One and the multiple is reminiscent of those Babylonian cosmologies, in which we find the demiurge joining battle with chaos.... We find then in Teilhard what amounts to a metaphysical mythology...[13]

While some basis for Tresmontant's interpretation may be found in the First World War essays which he cites, he is too eager to find analogies between Teilhard's position and mythological creation stories. We have tried to show that Teilhard was attempting, not always with the greatest felicity, to work out an understanding of the pre-creational state in conformity with his system, but also, and what is more important, in the context of the *Christian* notion of creation *ex nihilo*. Tresmontant's interpretation has been by and large endorsed by some other theologians, notably Charles Journet[14] and Piet Smulders.[15]

The essential orthodoxy, if not always the mode of expression, of Teilhard's argument has, on the other hand, been defended by Henri de Lubac,[16] Madeleine Barthélemy-Madaule,[17] Adolf Haas,[18]

Georges Crespy,[19] and Emile Rideau.[20] Respecting Teilhard's oft-repeated intention to remain strictly within the framework of the Christian doctrine of creation, these commentators, while in varying degrees critical of Teilhard's approach, see value in the efforts which he made. As the argument of this study unfolds in greater detail, it will become clearer why Teilhard found it quite impossible to think of the pre-creational state in any other terms. It will also become clearer that this rather difficult and admittedly tentative aspect of Teilhard's total thought coheres with the whole of his system and indeed sheds light on it.

The Initial Creation

The notion of a creation out of pure multiplicity gives rise to a picture of the initial creation quite different from that with which we are familiar from the Christian tradition, based as it is on the narrative in Genesis. The Genesis narrative presents us with the coming to be in a very brief interval of time of a world very similar to the world of our own experience. The world of Genesis is a highly structured one in which peace and serenity reign. It is a world which exists but briefly without knowing the influence of man's presence. It is a world which comes ready-made from the hand of God. The Book of Genesis knows of no genuine history of the world of nature previous to the appearance of man. The world of nature constitutes essentially a backdrop for the dramatic action which is man's history, the only history with which the Bible is really concerned. The world of Genesis in the space of a mere "week" seems to have come a very long distance from the nothingness out of which it was created. It is difficult to imagine such a world lapsing back into that nothingness from which it originated through the power of God, for this is a sturdy and apparently quite stable world. Finally, the world of Genesis is a world without evil, for once having created it God saw that it was good, indeed that it was very good.

It is hard to imagine an account which could give more vivid expression to the power of God. Creation is in Genesis a mighty and magnificent act of a great and all-powerful God. It would further be difficult to imagine an account which could more succinctly bring the reader to the heart of the dramatic action—the encounter between the unwaveringly faithful God and his unfaithful creature man. The stage is set with a succinctness of considerable artistry and the action joined with but a minimum of delay.

Nothing, on the contrary, could be less magnificent than the picture of the initial state of creation given us by Teilhard on the basis of scientific theory. As he says in an essay of 1919:

Owing to the fact that the most material form of being is also the closest to what is "purely unifiable," *concrete matter* will make its initial appearance in the form of *supreme dispersion.* The primordial state of the cosmos, by virtue of its materiality, is therefore to be conceived of as that of an extreme multiplicity, diffusion, and distension.[21]

In other words, since the initial state of creation is not far removed from the pre-creational state of pure multiplicity, it must of necessity take the form of an extreme multiplicity, already unified to some infinitesimal degree but also exhibiting a tendency to lapse back into non-being or pure multiplicity. The hold of the initial creation on existence is indeed tenuous. The initial creative act of God, in Teilhard's view, involves then a reduction of a possibly existing pure multiplicity to an actually existing extreme multiplicity. It would be difficult to imagine a less pretentious or more precarious inauguration of the created world.

The difference between Teilhard's account of creation and the narrative in Genesis is almost total in every respect. In the Genesis narrative, for example, we noted a complete lack of interest in the history of nature as such. For the redactor of Genesis, while the world of nature is a mighty and magnificent work of God, it serves primarily as a backdrop for the human drama which begins with the encounter between Adam and God. Teilhard, on the other hand, is profoundly interested in the history of nature, and his is a world which will not know the presence of man for billions of years. Perhaps the profoundest difference between Teilhard's view and the traditional understanding of creation, however, lies in the fact that for Teilhard creation is not primarily an act in the past at all. In fact, Teilhard is not particularly interested in the initial act of creation or in the initial state of creation. This diffidence arises out of a general principle of Teilhard's thought which holds that the true explanation of things is not to be discovered through an investigation of their origins. He states the principle himself as follows:

We instinctively tend to think that it is by working further and further backwards in time that we move closer and closer to the ultimate intelligibility of the world. Such an impression is nothing more than a delusion. In point of fact, things are least comprehensible at their origin. Like the river which gradually becomes smaller and smaller until it disappears altogether in the mire by the time that one arrives at its source, being becomes increasingly attenuated to the point of disappearing altogether when we attempt to divide it spatially into increasingly minute particles, or (what amounts to the same thing) when we attempt to situate it further and further backwards in time. The true greatness of a river is only comprehensible at its mouth, not at its source.[22]

Teilhard is interested primarily in the shape of the movement of creation, and the shape of any movement only becomes apparent after an immense span of time which is to be numbered in millions of years. Teilhard is in reality *most* deeply interested in the goal of the movement inasmuch as the end of the process constitutes the zone of maximum intelligibility. It is clear, then, why Teilhard shows no great interest in creation as an act or a state in the remote past. However, there is a still profounder reason for this and it serves to indicate the remarkable reversal of perspective which Teilhard's viewpoint introduces.

Creation is a continuing process for Teilhard and hence it cannot be equated with an act at the beginning of time, or more accurately, with an act which inaugurates the flow of time. God is continually creating; he was creating in the past and is still creating in the present and will continue to create in the future. Although Teilhard's concept of the initial creation as an extreme multiplicity would seem to denigrate God's creative power (particularly when juxtaposed with the Genesis narrative), the fact of the matter is that Teilhard's view postulates a gradual revelation of God's creative power. God's creative power is more evident in the present than it was in the past and the end of creation will of necessity constitute the supreme revelation of this creative power. Nothing (including God's creative power) is truly comprehensible for Teilhard except as viewed from the end, even if the shape of the end can be grasped to a limited extent from the shape of the movement towards the end as it begins to manifest itself on an immense time graph.

An Evolving Creation
and the Theory of Creative Union

In a view of creation which emphasizes an act in the past which brings into existence a world in most respects like the world of our own experience (especially with respect to the dimension of nature), it seems more appropriate to speak of God's conservation of his creation rather than to speak of a continuing creation. For Teilhard, on the other hand, the world is in process of being created through a gradual unification of multiplicity. Hence it is not so much a matter of conserving what is already in existence as of creating something new out of what already exists. Consequently, in Teilhard's view of things, evolution is the form which creation takes in a scientific world view: "Evolution is not really creative as science at one time thought; rather it is the expression, in terms of our own experience, of creation as it unfolds in space and time."[23] Teilhard very likely has in mind the title of Bergson's *Evolution créatrice*[24] (*Creative Evolution*) in this text, and he wishes to dissociate himself from this particular way of expressing the relationship between creation and evolution. In place of Bergson's formula *évolution créatrice* Teilhard later substituted his own formula *création évolutive*[25] (evolutionary creation), thus indicating that evolution is the form which creation assumes as far as our own experience of it is concerned. However, it is Teilhard's very earliest attempt to reformulate Bergson's *évolution créatrice* which is of particular interest at the moment, for it leads directly into Teilhard's earliest efforts at thinking through the notion of a continuous creation expressed in the form of an evolutionary process.

In 1917 Teilhard situated his own, as yet inchoate, theory of evolution vis-à-vis Bergson's in the following way:

While in Bergson's theory of creative evolution the cosmos is conceived of as a divergent movement springing from a center of radiation, the figure of the universe discovered by the theory of "creative union" is that of a centripetal movement from an infinitely distended sphere towards a center by way of reduction, convergence, and confluence. Although both theories are equally evolutionary in character, they are nonetheless diametrically opposed to one another.[26]

Teilhard resorts to the use of a geometrical model to make clear the difference between himself and Bergson. According to Teilhard, Bergson's theory of creative evolution involves a centrifugal movement away from the center of a circle by way of divergence, while his own theory of creative union involves a centripetal movement towards the center of a circle by way of convergence. The one theory sees evolution as a movement of expansion, the other as a movement of compression. The opposition between the two could hardly be more radical. To express this opposition Teilhard chooses the formula "creative union" to replace Bergson's "creative evolution." But what exactly does Teilhard mean by "creative union"?

In the essay from which we have just quoted the above, Teilhard offers this working description of what he means:

A union which is genuinely ontological (and of course it is absolutely necessary to grasp the full force of this term in order to comprehend what I am saying) is properly speaking creative. Creation takes place through a process of unification; and true union comes about only through creation. These two propositions are correlative.[27]

Reflecting further on the notion of creative union in 1924, Teilhard offers this more extended description:

Creative union is the theory which holds that in the present evolutionary phase of the cosmos (the only phase of course which is known to us), everything occurs in such a way that it appears as if the one were formed by means of successive unifications of the multiple. In other words, it appears as if the perfection of the one were in direct proportion to its capacity to center within itself in a more perfect way a larger multiplicity. For the elements grouped together by the soul into a body (and by that very fact elevated to a superior level of being) "*plus esse est plus cum pluribus uniri.*" For the soul itself, which is the principle of unity, "*plus esse est plus plura unire.*" For both of them, to receive or to communicate union is to undergo the creative influence of God "*qui creat uniendo.*"[28]

If all the details of this obviously important text are not immediately transparent, the general thrust of it is at least fairly plain. Teilhard uses the example of the relationship between the body and the soul to illustrate his point, but his remarks are intended to cover all the varied manifestations of the matter/spirit relationship observable during the whole course of evolution. In terms of the body/soul

illustration actually chosen by Teilhard, the body (or matter) functions as that which is unified, and the soul (or spirit) functions as
that which unifies. That which is unified and that which unifies
are then said to undergo the creative influence of God who creates
by uniting. In other words, the soul, while itself a principle of
unification, is not the ultimate principle of unification, since this
function belongs only to God. Nothing is said of the type of
causality to be attributed to God's creative (or unifying) activity or
what respective roles are to be allotted to the unifying power of the
soul and the unifying power of God. Later, in Chapter VI, we
shall see how Teilhard attempted to deal with the problem of
causality in terms of his theory of creative union, but for the
moment this question is not crucial to the development of Teilhard's
argument.

The theory of creative union, as an attempt to come to grips with
the problem of an evolving creation, is crystallized in a formula
which we have already met: to create is to unite.[29] As he himself
says: *"Deus creat uniendo."*[30] God creates by unifying. Teilhard,
in working out his theory of creative union, takes his point of
departure from the assumption that it is God who creates. In fact,
he explicitly rejects the possibility that the multiple is self-creative
of unity:

Of and by itself, the multiple is quite incapable of grouping itself together and of thus making progress in being, for it is simply a power of
dispersion (i.e. of annihilation). Under such conditions, there is
obviously no need to accept the untenable hypothesis of a multiplicity
which finds within itself the principle of its own unification.[31]

Hence, moving from the field of a faith which accepts the reality of
God as the ultimate creative principle, Teilhard enters the field
of phenomenological observation on the basis of which he delineates
the movement of evolution as a process of unification. Teilhard
then, *as a believing scientist*, comes to the conclusion that the
process of evolutionary unification observable by a phenomenological methodology, constitutes the modality of God's creative
activity as far as we are able to grasp that activity in experience.
In other words, it *seems* to us that God creates by unifying the
multiple.

To conclude this preliminary description of what Teilhard means by the theory of creative union, we should like to underline once again the fact that for Teilhard all of created reality is dipolar in structure, constituted by that which is unified and that which unifies. That which has no principle of unity and hence has in no way been unified is pure multiplicity and is equivalent to non-being. Thus the dialectical or dipolar relationship between the passive and active constituents of reality only begins with the initial act of creation itself. Teilhard himself characterizes the dipolar structure of beings in terms of activity and passivity. Creative union takes, then, an active and a passive form which Teilhard generally expresses in the two Latin phrases: *"plus esse est plus cum pluribus uniri"* (passive form) and *"plus esse est plus plura unire"* (active form).[32] These may be translated respectively as follows: to be more is to be better united with a greater number of elements (passive form) and to be more is to better unite a greater number of elements (active form). Teilhard himself freely translates the sense of the formulas thusly: "to be = to unite oneself or to unite others" (active form) and "to be = to be united and unified by another" (passive form).[33]

Teilhard's own translation indicates the broad extension which the theory of creative union is intended to have. In short, the whole of created reality is dipolar in structure, either actively uniting or passively undergoing unification. The whole movement of creation is summed up for Teilhard in this dialectic. The relationship between matter and spirit, the individual and the totality of humanity, and God and the world, all fall under the law of creative union in its active and passive forms, as we shall see in subsequent chapters. Even Teilhardian spirituality, centered as it is on the complementarity of activity and passivity, is an outgrowth of the theory of creative union. While explicit references to creative union comprise but a relatively small fraction of the vast corpus of Teilhard's writings, the notion itself lies at the heart of Teilhard's entire system.[34] Teilhard came upon the theory of creative union early in his career, and the remainder of his life was spent in refining its expression and its implications. While he later found better terms in which to formulate the various aspects of the theory of creative union, the basic lines of his system are already contained in the First World War essays which constitute a sustained effort over a period of four years to arrive at and to explicitate the theory of creative union.

In a letter written to his cousin Marguerite Teillard-Chambon in 1952, Teilhard says of these essays: "My papers from the War may well be psychologically interesting for anyone wishing to study the ontogenesis of an idea, but they contain nothing which I have not said in a clearer way since then."[35] In point of fact, however, the First World War essays possess more than a merely psychological interest, for it seems quite impossible to understand the profoundest intentions of Teilhard's later work apart from a careful reading of these early attempts to formulate his world view. The remaining chapters of this study are not intended as an apologia for this assertion, but rather they are intended to trace the development of the theory of creative union during and after the First World War. We hope to be able to show that it provides a key, perhaps *the* key, for understanding Teilhard de Chardin's system of thought, for it was by means of the theory of creative union that Teilhard sought to resolve the problem of the one and the many.

Summary

We may now summarize the results of our investigation up to this point before proceeding to explore in greater detail the various ramifications of Teilhard's theory of creative union. We have focused in this chapter on Teilhard's overall treatment of the problem of creation, in its pre-creational state of pure multiplicity, its initial state of extreme multiplicity, and its evolving state of multiplicity undergoing unification. We have seen that Teilhard derives his notion of pure multiplicity, equivalent in fact to non-being, from both a deductive analysis of trinitization and an inductive inspection of the evolutionary movement as a movement of unification. Pure multiplicity thus becomes the logical antipode of God's trinitarian unity, while the trinitarian unity becomes the archetypal pattern and goal of multiplicity's unification. We have, moreover, seen that Teilhard's efforts to find a rational ground beyond God's love, upon which to base God's commitment to creation, rests upon a faulty understanding of love, probably influenced by the nominalistic notion of God's *potentia absoluta*. Teilhard clearly wishes to affirm creation *ex nihilo* at the same time that he wishes to avoid any hint that creation is a merely arbitrary act on God's part, a matter of indifference to him.

Finally, we have seen that for Teilhard creation is a continuous process involving the unification of multiplicity. The theory of creative union, in both its active and passive forms, seeks to render an account of this notion of an evolving creation in the formula "to create is to unite." Both that which unites (spirit) and that which is united (matter) undergo the creative influence of God who creates by uniting. In this first chapter, then, we have been concerned with a preliminary elaboration of the theory of creative union in relationship to the problem of creation in its most general aspects. Having in this way provided a skeletal outline of the origin and movement of creation in terms of unity and multiplicity, we should now like to begin to flesh out this skeletal framework in terms of the relationship between matter and spirit.

2

Matter and Spirit

The problem of the one and the many, as we observed at the beginning of the previous chapter, is a threefold problem for Teilhard. In this chapter we should like to consider the first aspect of this problem: the relationship between spirit (the one) and matter (the many). We shall focus our attention particularly on the spirit/matter relationship as it is developed in the specific context of the theory of creative union, but we should also like to show how this relationship is elaborated in other contexts and how these in turn cohere with the theory of creative union.

The Context of Creative Union

We begin with a text of capital importance from an essay entitled "Mon Univers" and written in 1924, in which Teilhard discusses the origin of the theory of creative union in the perplexing problematic of the spirit/matter relationship:

The theory of creative union is not so much a metaphysical doctrine as a sort of empirical and pragmatic explanation of the universe. This theory came to birth out of my own personal need to reconcile, within the confines of a rigorously structured system, the views of science respecting evolution (which views are accepted here as being definitively established, at least in their essence) with an innate tendency which has driven me to seek out the presence of God, not apart from the physical world, but rather through matter and in a certain sense in union with it.

I arrived at the theory of creative union in a quite simple way as a result of my own personal reflections on the rather disconcerting relationships which obtain between spirit and matter. Experience has made it incontrovertibly evident to me that "the psychic capacities of all the living things of which we have any knowledge are intimately bound up with the degree of organic complexity involved." The spirituality of the soul appears to be directly proportional to the multiplicity and fragility of the body. Unfortunately, this somewhat curious law of correlation does not seem to have attracted the attention of philosophers. When they have noticed this interrelationship at all, they have always seized upon it as another opportunity to widen still further the gulf which they are only too happy to fix between spirit and matter. For my own part, it seems to me that, far from being merely paradoxical or accidental, this relationship very likely betrays the inner make-up of beings. Consequently, I have chosen to make of this relationship a principle of explanation rather than to see it as a difficulty or an objection.[1]

Teilhard then goes on to speak in the following paragraph of the relationship between matter and spirit in terms of passivity and activity. We have already discussed this text in the first chapter and need not detain ourselves over it here. The important qualifications which Teilhard adds to this text, however, are crucial for a proper understanding of his point, and thus we may resume the thread of his argument with these:

These formulas have to be carefully weighed lest they be misunderstood. They are not intended to convey the impression that the one is simply composed of the multiple, that is to say, that the one comes to birth by means of the fusion within itself of the various elements which it associates together. If such were the case, then nothing would in fact be created, since nothing new would appear. Furthermore, if such were the case, the multiple would progressively reduce itself to unity, which is obviously contrary to experience. Hence, the theory of creative union simply seeks to account for the fact that the one appears only in conjunction with multiplicity and that the one dominates multiplicity inasmuch as its essential, formal function is to unite. Consequently, we are led to the formulation of the following principle: "Creative union does not confuse together the elements which it groups into a unity (does not the beauty of such a theory consist precisely in the fact that it allows the one to be united to that which is other while remaining what it is?). Creative union does not only conserve the elements thus associated together, but rather brings them to fulfillment, as can be seen in the case of living bodies in which the specialization of the cells is directly proportional to their degree of elevation within the animal series. The more elevated the soul, the better it differentiates the elements which it unites."[2]

The theory of creative union seeks, in the first place, to call attention to the phenomenologically observable fact that the psychic capacities of the soul[3] are profoundly conditioned by the degree of complexification of the material elements involved in the union. The ascending curve of the spiritualization of the universe can be observed to be a function of the ascending curve of the complexification of matter which thus serves as the base for spiritualization. Lest the reader be tempted to read into this relationship the unwarranted conclusion that the spiritual pole of reality results simply from the fusion of the multiplicity of matter, Teilhard goes on, in the second place, to obviate such a misunderstanding. The appearance of the spiritual pole is always conditioned by the degree of complexification of the material pole, but the former is never merely the product of the latter. The spiritual is not reducible to its material base. If it were, the multiple would be shown to be self-unitive and the structure of the world would then in fact turn out to be monopolar. Teilhard's dipolar theory of creative union does indeed demand a respect for the function of the material base, but it also argues for the primacy of the spirit which is the principle of unity of the material base and not just its accidental by-product.

The theory of creative union as expressed in these texts of 1924 already contains germinally what will later become the well-known law of complexity-consciousness and the equally well-known formula "*l'union différencie*" ("union differentiates"). However, before moving ahead in time to an examination of these developments, we must first move backwards in time to the First World War essays to see what Teilhard made of the spirit/matter relationship in his earliest formulations of the theory of creative union.

We may appropriately begin with "La Lutte contre la multitude," written in the early months of 1917, since it already adumbrates the general approach of "L'Union créatrice," written towards the end of the same year, although Teilhard had not as yet arrived at the formula "creative union" to describe his position. Having spoken of the unification of multiplicity which of necessity had to precede the appearance of life, he goes on to say that:

Psychic simplicity, such as we know it, is born of multiplicity. It comes to flower out of the soil of organic complexification, a complexification involving a hard-won victory over a far-flung kingdom of multiplicity. Proportionate to the multiplicity which has been unified within it, organically complexified matter will of necessity be subject to a maximal tendency towards decomposition. The soul is created by virtue of the degree of materiality which it is able to group and coordinate together. The life of the soul is, then, intimately bound up with the degree of complexified matter which it has successfully brought under its dominion and unifying power.[4]

The same line of argument is repeated in "L'Union créatrice."[5] Teilhard is clearly having trouble in this text avoiding the conclusion that evolution is a soul-making process, although in point of fact he wants the evolution of matter to be understood as a soul-conditioning process. In the following year, he himself acknowledges that he is not too happy with the theory of creative union as it applies "to the formation of the soul." He then adds this important qualifying observation: "My aim in attempting to reduce everything to the notion of union has not been so much to find a metaphysical solution to the riddle of the universe, but rather to discover an historical and practical form for the developments of creation."[6] This text marks an important transition in the development of the theory of creative union as it applies to the matter/spirit relationship in that it frees the theory from metaphysical considerations of dubious value. It thus allows the theory of creative union to function as an "empirical law of phenomena," which seeks not to resolve the difficult question of causality, but rather to give shape to the process of evolution as a movement of spiritualization intimately bound up with the concomitant and conditioning movement of material complexification. By giving shape to the movement of evolution, the theory of creative union also provides a sense of meaning and direction to evolution. Evolution is a movement directed towards the growth of the spiritual pole of the universe, the pole of unity. And matter's role in this movement is ultimately reducible to a service function; matter provides the steps on which spirit will ascend ever higher.

It is this break in 1918 with the metaphysical pretensions of the theory of creative union that will lead at a later stage to the law of complexity-consciousness. This law had not yet achieved formulation in 1924 when "Mon Univers" was written. However, as we saw at the beginning of the chapter, the texts of "Mon Univers" already reveal an earnest effort to avoid the ambiguities of earlier formulations and to underline in the clearest possible way the distinction between matter and spirit (in terms of activity and passivity) without at the same time creating an unbridgeable dualism between them. We now turn our attention to the problem of the interrelationship between matter and spirit as it ultimately found expression in the law of complexity-consciousness.

The Law of Complexity-Consciousness

In "Le Coeur de la matière," an essay delineating the stages in Teilhard's intellectual autobiography, we are told that as late as 1930 the law of complexity-consciousness had not yet distinctly made its appearance.[7] However, as we have already seen, the rudiments of this crucially important concept were clearly present in Teilhard's attempt to work out the notion of creative union during the First World War. This can be readily seen from a comparison of Teilhard's mature formulations of the law of complexity-consciousness with the texts which have already been discussed from the earlier essays. In *The Phenomenon of Man*, for example, Teilhard has this to say of complexity-consciousness:

The degree of concentration of a consciousness, we may now say, is inversely proportional to the simplicity of the material composite to which it corresponds. Or to state the same point more positively: the degree of perfection of a consciousness is directly proportional to the richness of organization of the material base to which it corresponds.

Spiritual perfection (or conscious "centration") and material synthesis (or "complexity") are simply the two sides or interrelated parts of the same phenomenon.[8]

In a note to this text Teilhard attempts to elucidate his meaning by means of a geometrical model:

From this point of view, one could say that every being is structured (phenomenologically speaking) in the form of an ellipse with two intimately related foci: a focus of material organization and a focus of psychic centration. These two foci vary in the very same sense in strict solidarity with one another.

The image of the ellipse illustrates with admirable clarity what we previously termed the "dipolar structure of beings" at the same time that it underlines the intimate relationship between the mutual development of the conjoined poles.

The year following the completion of *The Phenomenon of Man*, Teilhard returns to the same point:

I am not seeking to arrive at a definition of the nature of either spirit or matter. My point (and it depends on nothing more than phenomenological observation) is simply that the most important discovery made in this century is very likely the recognition of the fact that the movement of history may be most accurately measured in terms of a gradual gathering together of matter into increasingly well structured groupings, whose ever richer and better centrated arrangement is accompanied by an increasingly apparent growth of freedom and interiority. The phenomenon of developing consciousness on the earth is, in short, directly proportional to the increasingly advanced organization of more highly complexified elements, brought about in successive moments by the efforts of life chemistry. For the time being at least, I can see no more satisfactory solution of the enigma presented to us by the physical progress of the universe.[9]

As Teilhard himself says in the same paragraph, "there is nothing metaphysical in all this." The law of complexity-consciousness is arrived at by means of a phenomenological methodology, which is concerned with "nothing other than the phenomenon, but nonetheless the phenomenon in its totality."[10]

Little would be gained by following the development of Teilhard's formulation of the law of complexity-consciousness beyond the texts which we have already noted, since the later texts only serve to refine further what is already clear enough for our purposes. The law of complexity-consciousness is, in its root meaning, a law of correlation, which seeks to articulate the mutual interdependence of matter and spirit in the overall movement of evolution. Starting from the premise that reality is essentially dipolar in structure and that matter and spirit are not antagonistic to one another but rather constitute complementary principles in the construction of being, the law of complexity-consciousness assigns to matter the role of conditioning the appearance of spirit— the level of spiritualization being directly proportional to the degree of complexification of the matter involved in the composite. So intimate is the relationship between matter and spirit for Teilhard that he does not hesitate to speak of matter as "the matrix of consciousness" and of consciousness as being "born from the womb of matter."[11] In fact Teilhard is not even afraid to speak of matter becoming spirit.[12] Such expressions, at first sight, seem unduly ambiguous in the context of the law of complexity-consciousness which is quite circumspect in its attempt to articulate the distinction between matter and spirit albeit without separation or opposition. Such expressions undoubtedly do serve, however, to emphasize the correlation between matter and spirit in a striking way, and they seem quite valid at the level of purely phenomenological observation.

For Teilhard, matter and spirit are not two things which by some device or other have to be glued together into a unity. Rather, matter and spirit are similar to two foci of the same ellipse, they are aspects of all created being, ultimately distinguishable but not separable. In fact, as the law of complexity-consciousness indicates, the complexity of the one conditions the status of the other. Precisely in order to avoid the impression that matter is a thing which could exist apart from a spiritual pole, Teilhard in his later writings frequently resorted to the German expression "*Weltstoff*" or its French equivalent "*l'étoffe de l'univers*" ("the stuff of the universe") to indicate by the very imprecision of the term itself that the basic components of the universe are dipolar in structure and not simply material.[13] "There is in the world neither spirit nor matter: the 'stuff of the universe' is rather *spirit-matter*. No other type of substance could ultimately lead to the human molecule."[14] For Teilhard, the concept of pure matter would be equivalent to pure multiplicity or non-being. So convinced of the dipolarity of created being was Teilhard that in his earliest essays he was quite willing to entertain the idea of some kind of attenuated materiality even for the angels.[15] Since it has already become quite clear that the basic thrust of Teilhard's mind is towards unity, it is not surprising to find that he makes every effort to overcome the long-standing dichotomous dualism between matter and spirit. It is pertinent to ask more precisely, however, how one distinguishes these two poles within such a unitary world view.

Matter and Spirit as Directional Vectors of the Evolutionary Movement

"The two processes of which we have spoken (that is spiritualization and materialization) are rigorously bound up with one another in the movement of evolution inasmuch as they constitute the two faces of the same thing."[16] These two faces of reality may also be considered as two poles:

Historically as well as scientifically, "the greater" presupposes "the less." Consequently, spirit and matter, ordinarily regarded as two antagonistic universes which have been associated together in some quite incomprehensible way, are in fact only two poles united by a flux. Throughout the movement of this flux the elements, however different ontologically one may care to suppose them to be, can only make their appearance within a zone, i.e. in a clearly determined order. Strictly speaking, this law of distribution is valid only in terms of appearances.[17]

Phenomenologically speaking, then, matter and spirit constitute but two aspects (faces or poles) of the same thing, or rather the same process of growing complexity and consciousness. A phenomenological methodology is able to break down the great wall of separation erected between matter and spirit and thus destroy any dualism of opposition between matter and spirit. Is Teilhard's position, phenomenologically considered at least, reducible, then, to a simple monism?

We have already seen that Teilhard distinguishes between matter and spirit in terms of complexity and simplicity (the law of complexity-consciousness) and in terms of passivity and activity (the theory of creative union). However, he also attempts to establish a certain duality between them by treating them as directional vectors of the movement of reality.

It is no longer possible within the context of the theory of creative union to continue to promote a dichotomous opposition between spirit and matter. For the man who has really grasped the meaning of the law of "spiritualization through union," there can no longer exist two watertight compartments in the universe, that of spirits and that of bodies. In fact, these are now seen to be but two directions along the very same road (the direction of pluralization and the direction of unification, the one being the wrong direction, and hence evil, and the other being the right direction and hence good. . . .

Matter and spirit are not to be set in opposition to one another as two things or two natures, but rather as the two directions of evolution within the world.[18]

The same point is made in 1936 in the context of the problem of the one and the many:

There really exists no genuine antinomy between the one and the many if one takes the trouble to see things in the context of a flux of personalization. Rather, the one and the many are simply two phases (or more accurately two directions) of the same reality in movement all around us.[19]

Teilhard's view of matter and spirit as directional vectors strikes a death blow at every form of Manichaeism, and this is precisely its intention. "Do not say any longer that matter is condemned, that matter is evil."[20] Matter is not intrinsically evil as Manichaeism maintains, rather it is ambivalent, it possesses both good and evil possibilities which depend upon the direction in which matter, or more accurately the stuff of the universe, is moving. Or to put it another way, it depends upon the fecundity of matter, the matrix of spirit. As matter becomes more and more elaborately complexified, it gives birth to more and more elevated forms of spirit—matter is good, it is the great mother pregnant with spirit. As matter is increasingly pulverized into more and more minute and diverse forms of multiplicity, it becomes increasingly sterile—matter is evil, it is the barren woman who makes abortion the law of the universe. Teilhard's attitude to matter is not naïvely optimistic; he knows of the evil possibilities of matter. He refers to matter in this sense as evil matter, or dead matter, or inverted matter, or matter understood in a material or carnal way,[21] but he always means by it matter which is moving in the direction of multiplicity.

The precise point of what Teilhard is saying may be seen more clearly by returning to the notion of *Weltstoff*. *Weltstoff*, or the stuff of the universe, is elliptical or dipolar in structure, and as it is unified the material focus or pole is complexified with the result that the spiritual focus or pole is intensified. Looking at the same movement from the opposite direction, one may observe that "as one moves backwards into the past of the cosmos, the variable of spirit continually diminishes, but like an asymptote, it will never completely disappear." [22] The movement of evolution, seen over an immense span of time, gives the appearance of matter passing into or becoming spirit. Claude Cuénot sums up the point well:

Teilhard's view is fundamentally monistic; however, Teilhard holds on to a certain dualism which he subordinates to this basic monism. Or, to change the metaphor, matter and spirit, as poles of the very same *Weltstoff*, constitute two vectors moving in opposite directions. [23]

It is this understanding of matter and spirit as two directions of the movement of evolution which serves to clarify Teilhard's understanding of the sacred and the profane:

Properly speaking, there is nothing which is sacred or profane, pure or impure. Rather, there is only a good or an evil direction: on the one hand, the direction of ascent, of enriching unification, of greater spiritual effort; and on the other hand, the direction of descent, of impoverishing egoism, of materialistic pleasure-seeking. Followed in the direction which leads upwards, all creatures become luminous, while followed in the direction which leads downwards, they become opaque, indeed demonic. [24]

"Matter is not the stable foundation of the world," [25] rather it is spirit which holds the primacy, everything holds together from above, [26] not from below. "For the man who knows how to see correctly, the analysis of matter reveals the priority, the primacy of spirit." [27]

Teilhard was constantly working towards an integral interpretation of the relationship between matter and spirit in order to establish a cogent position beyond what he considered to be the sterile debate between materialists and spiritualists. [28] For Teilhard, "spirit is neither a meta- nor an epiphenomenon: it is rather *the* phenomenon." [29] He does not attempt to demonstrate the primacy of spirit by means of a specifically philosophical argument or by trying to locate it within a static hierarchy of being. Rather, the primacy of spirit becomes discernible to the man who knows how to see things aright in terms of the directionality of an evolutionary movement, whose meaning lies in the genesis of spirit out of complexifying matter.

The conception of matter and spirit as two directions of the same process is closely tied in with several other themes of Teilhard's thought which serve to elucidate what he means by this conception. Through a brief analysis of these related themes, it will be possible to indicate still more clearly how Teilhard views the movement of evolution as a struggle between the forces of unification and the forces of dispersion. At the same time, it will help to illuminate further the relationship between matter and spirit as Teilhard sees it.

Analysis and Synthesis

We may begin our exposition of these related themes with Teilhard's understanding of the relationship between analysis and synthesis.

When we want to know what is in a room we open the door; when we want to know what is in a watch, we take it apart; when we want to know what is inside a nut, we break it open. When we want to find out what a thing is made up of, we instinctively set about analyzing it by taking it apart. From this instinctive tendency of the human mind the whole of science has issued, for science is essentially a work of analysis. The method, as well as the conclusions, of scientific research are dominated by the principle that the secret of things lies in their elementary constituents. Consequently, according to such a view of science, in order to understand the world, it is sufficient to get back to the most simple elements out of which the world has emerged.[30]

This text from 1921 is echoed in *The Phenomenon of Man:*

Modern man is obsessed by the need to depersonalize (or impersonalize) all that he most admires. There are two reasons for this tendency. The first is analysis—that wonderful instrument of scientific research, to which we are indebted for all our advances, but which at the same time, by breaking down synthesis after synthesis, allows one soul after another to escape, thus leaving us with but a pile of dismantled machinery and evanescent particles.[31]

Teilhard clearly recognized that science had identified itself with an analytic approach "for perfectly legitimate reasons of both utility and methodology."[32] He never contested the fact that such an approach had yielded impressive results. What he did contest, however, was the implicit assumption that an analytic methodology was capable of rendering a satisfactory account of the meaning of the universe. The meaning of anything, as we have already seen, can only be grasped for Teilhard by following its course within the ascending movement of evolution, not by attempting to situate it retrogressively further and further backwards in the history of the universe. If the movement of evolution is in fact a movement of synthetic unification, then its meaning can only be grasped by a synthetic act of understanding. The one method (analysis) is committed to following the movement of evolution in the direction of decomposition and multiplicity, whereas the other (synthesis) is committed to following the movement of evolution in the direction of composition and unification. Hence, the method of analysis will be concerned almost exclusively with the material pole of things, what Teilhard refers to as the "without of things," while the method of synthesis will be concerned primarily with the spiritual pole of things, what Teilhard refers to as the "within of things." However, if analysis can safely ignore the within of things and still achieve brilliant practical results, synthesis cannot with impunity ignore the complexification of the without of things and still achieve a balanced understanding of the meaning of evolution.

In a method dominated by synthetic understanding, the primacy of the spirit over matter is equivalent to the primacy of the future over the past.[33] The direction of matter revealed by analysis is towards multiplicity and the past. The direction of spirit revealed by synthesis is towards unity and the future. The choice of methodological perspective, then, conditions what the observer sees and the whole of Teilhard's system is directed towards vision. All of Teilhard's writings are an invitation to see the world from the perspective of unitary synthesis:

Without any concern, for the moment at least, to safeguard in my mode of expression the tenets of any particular school of orthodoxy (whether it be scientific or religious)—and yet with an acute awareness of acting only through a total fidelity to my double vocation as a man and as a Christian—I would like to help others to see the breathtaking vision which I have seen by means of what is after all but a rather simple change of perspective.

I am not pushing a thesis of any kind; rather, what I offer is my own personal witness, or, if one prefers, I am offering an invitation. The invitation of a traveler who, having left the beaten track, has quite by chance stumbled upon a point of view from which everything suddenly becomes strikingly luminous, and who calls out to his companions: "Come and see."[34]

The words of Robert Frost apply admirably to Teilhard:

> Two roads diverged in a wood, and I—
> I took the one less traveled by,
> And that has made all the difference.[35]

Tangential and Radial Energy

According to the law of complexity-consciousness, matter and spirit represent the two interdependent variables or poles which constitute the basic structure of all created reality. For Teilhard, matter is the great mother figure of the evolutionary movement, for from her womb spirit is born. But, in the last analysis, the mother's role is one of self-effacement—it is the child who is to hold the primacy. "He must increase, but I must decrease" (John 3, 30). From within a fundamentally monistic view of the relationship between matter and spirit, there emerges a duality of direction which postulates not only the primacy of spirit over matter, but also the primacy of unity over multiplicity and of the future over the past. Such a directional duality necessitates a methodological change of perspective from analysis to synthesis in order to grasp the meaning of the overall movement of evolution as a movement of unification through greater spiritualization.

Bound up with the theme of matter and spirit as directional vectors is the theme of tangential and radial energy which we must now explore in order to fill out further the picture which Teilhard has already drawn for us. The terms "radial" and "tangential" as such occur for the first time in *The Phenomenon of Man*, and Teilhard defines them there as follows:

So as to avoid a fundamental dualism, which would be both anti-scientific and ultimately impossible, and at the same time to safeguard the natural complexification of the stuff of the universe, I accordingly propose the following as a basis for all that is to emerge later.

We shall assume that all energy is essentially psychic in nature; but add that in each particular element this fundamental energy is divided into two distinct components: a *tangential energy* which links the element with all others of the same order (that is to say, of the same complexity and centreity) as itself in the universe; and a *radial energy* which draws it towards ever greater complexity and centreity—in other words forwards.[36]

On the basis of this definition Teilhard goes on to give the following picture:

From this initial state, supposing it has at its disposal a certain amount of free tangential energy, the particle thus constituted must obviously be in a position to increase its internal complexity in association with neighboring particles, and thereby (since its centreity is automatically increased) to augment its radial energy. The latter will then be able to react in turn in the domain of the tangential in the form of a new arrangement. And so on.[37]

Working from these texts, we may say that tangential and radial energy correspond to the material pole of complexification and the spiritual pole of consciousness respectively. Tangential energy is equivalent to the energy of complexification which conditions the growth of the pole of consciousness. However, the relationship between tangential and radial energy is no longer simply that of the passive relationship between engendering mother and engendered child. Rather, the child of complexification, that is spirit or consciousness or radial energy, also reacts on the mother, molds her as it were, in order that she might become more prolific. Tangential and radial energy thus interact to further complexify the material base which spirit requires to move forwards. This line of argument, by taking us beyond the purely passive character of spirit, establishes a dialectical movement of activity and passivity which recalls the theory of creative union.

What is disconcerting, however, is that the notion of tangential energy seems in no way to be related to the notion of matter as a directional vector orientated towards multiplicity and the past. Two observations may be made in this regard. First of all, while it is true that matter represents a tendency to dissolution, it is also true that this tendency is to some extent checked by its union with spirit. Matter is caught up in the dynamic thrust of spirit forwards and in this sense matter becomes spirit. Matter can be made to move in the direction of spirit even if its fundamental thrust is in the opposite direction. Tangential energy, considered from this positive point of view, underlines the role of complexified matter in the evolutionary genesis of spirit. Secondly, Teilhard does speak of a negative aspect to tangential energy which relates it more clearly to the notion of matter, as a directional force opposed to spirit.

Lastly, since, according to our reading, the entire edifice of the universe is constantly supported at every phase of its progressive "centration" by its primary arrangements, it is plain that its achievement will be conditioned up to the highest stages by a certain primordial quantum of free tangential energy, which will gradually exhaust itself, following the principle of entropy.[38]

The movement of complexification is a reversible one because of the effect of entropy, which represents the negative, descending aspect of tangential energy. We need not dwell on this here, as we shall presently have to consider the concept of entropy in greater detail.

The treatment of tangential and radial energy in *The Phenomenon of Man* constitutes a variation on the law of complexity-consciousness. As Teilhard says towards the close of that work: "the radial is a function of the tangential,"[39] just as he speaks of consciousness being a function of complexity. Since Teilhard generally uses the notions of tangential and radial energy in the context of the socialization of mankind, which is the subject of Chapter IV, we need not detain ourselves further here over this issue.

Entropy and the Movement of Life

Teilhard speaks of tangential energy as constant but reversible, while he speaks of radial energy as increasing and irreversible. In this section we wish to focus our attention on the reversible properties of tangential energy because of the relevance of this problem to Teilhard's understanding of matter and spirit as opposed directions of the evolutionary movement.

When Teilhard speaks of tangential energy as being both constant and reversible, he is referring to what he calls "the two major laws of the conservation and degradation of energy,"[40] the first two laws of thermodynamics. What this means is that while the amount of energy in the universe remains constant, the amount of *usable* energy in the universe is constantly on the decrease. In every transformation of energy from one form into another, a certain amount of heat energy is lost and becomes unavailable. In short, the amount of available energy in the universe is running down even if the amount of energy (available and unavailable) in the universe remains constant. According to the law of the degradation of energy (or the law of entropy), the movement of the universe is reversible and will gradually tend to return to a state of equilibrium or what Teilhard would term "a state of multiplicity." While science (particularly physics) recognizes only the existence of tangential energy because it is concerned only with the without of things, Teilhard introduces the notion of a radial energy which pertains to the within of things in order to establish a current of energy running in opposition to entropy.

We saw above that matter is an ambivalent factor in the growth of the world in that it can function either as the matrix out of which spirit emerges or as the direction towards multiplicity which suffocates spirit. The same ambivalence is observable with regard to tangential energy. However, with the notion of entropy we focus foursquare on the negative aspect of matter as a tendency to dissolution and decomposition. Furthermore, with the notion of entropy we enter into a new form of the dialectic between matter and spirit, that of the relationship between entropy and life. Epistemologically speaking, this new dialectic involves an attempt to adjudicate the tension between the perspective of physics and the point of view of biology. We may begin with a text written in 1928, the year when the contrast between entropy and life begins to make its appearance in Teilhard's writings, at least in a terminologically precise way.

Without in any way forsaking the domain or the methods of the sciences of matter, we already find ourselves in a position to make the observation that life, taken *in globo*, appears to be a current running in opposition to entropy. As we all know, entropy is the name given by science to that apparently inevitable tendency of corpuscular unities (in which are located all physico-chemical phenomena) to fall backwards, in virtue of the statistical laws of probability, in the direction of a median state of diffuse activity, a state in which every exchange of usable energy ceases as far as we are able to tell. Everything around us seems to be in process of descending towards this death of matter; everything that is, except life. Contrary to the leveling effect of entropy, life consists in the methodical and constantly broadening construction of an increasingly improbable edifice. Protozoa, metazoa, sociable animals, man, and humanity constitute so many acts of more and more blatant defiance of the law of entropy; so many increasingly striking exceptions to the general tendencies of energy and of chance.[41]

Teilhard speaks of "these two conjoined currents"[42] or "axes"[43] as the "two faces or directions of the same extremely generalized event."[44] They constitute "opposed poles"[45] of two inverse movements,[46] the one descending into the past towards the more probable, the other rising into the future towards the less probable.[47] Through the notions of entropy and life "science may be able to incorporate once again into its own perspective the ancient intuitions of some kind of cosmic dualism,"[48] for life may be defined negatively as a kind of anti-entropy or negative entropy.[49] It is even possible to describe the whole movement of evolution in terms of the declining primacy of entropy and the growing primacy of life.[50]

The notions which Teilhard has grouped together around the theme of entropy and life correspond in large measure with what we have already seen with regard to Teilhard's understanding of the relationship between matter and spirit, particularly when understood as two directions of the evolutionary movement. However, the scientific concept of entropy affords Teilhard a means of focusing directly on the negative aspect of matter and thus helps to clarify what he means by saying that matter is a direction towards decomposition and multiplicity. It highlights an aspect of the matter/spirit relationship with which the law of complexity-consciousness is unable to deal directly.

Summary

The notion of entropy and the general theme of matter as a direction opposed to spirit pointedly raise the problem of evil in an evolving universe, and it is to this problem that we must address ourselves in the next chapter. However, before proceeding further we may summarize the argument of the present chapter. We have attempted to show basically how Teilhard understands the spirit/matter relationship in terms of the problem of the one and the many. Beginning with the theory of creative union, understood not as a metaphysical theory but rather as "an empirical law of phenomena," we saw that the degree of matter's spiritualization appears to be directly proportional to its organic complexity. This insight is later developed by Teilhard into his well-known law of complexity-consciousness. We also saw that in terms of the theory of creative union spirit may be considered that which unifies (the one) while matter may be considered as that which is unified (the many). Matter and spirit thus become the passive and active poles or faces of the evolutionary movement, a movement of unification and spiritualization ascending to higher and higher forms of synthesis in the future.

Having in this way distinguished matter and spirit in terms of complexity and simplicity and passivity and activity, we then went on to distinguish them further as two directional vectors of the evolutionary movement, the one (matter) moving towards multiplicity in the past and the other (spirit) moving towards unity in the future. This particular approach to matter and spirit is, moreover, reflected in several other interconnected themes, namely the relationship between analysis and synthesis, tangential and radial energy, and entropy and life.

However, if it is true that matter possesses an intrinsic tendency to dissociation, it is also true that this tendency can be checked and even reversed to some extent by the association of matter with spirit, whose dynamic thrust is in the opposite direction. This fact will become increasingly important with the appearance of man, because man through his freedom will have it in his power to determine, to a large if not exclusive extent, the directionality of matter. But this is to anticipate a later chapter. What we wish to concentrate on at the moment is the negativity within the evolutionary movement, the tendency to dissolution, materialization, and multiplicity.

III

Involution and the Problem of Evil

Up to this point we have been considering Teilhard's attempted solution to the problem of the one and the many in the context of an evolving universe. We may now profitably summarize the results of our investigation into the modality of creation, as Teilhard understands it. Hypothesizing deductively from trinitization and inductively from the shape of the evolutionary movement as one of unification, Teilhard arrives at a notion of the pre-creational state as one of pure multiplicity, equivalent in fact to non-being. The initial act of creation consists in the positing of a state of extreme multiplicity which is destined subsequently to undergo a process of unification, the mode of God's continuous creative activity as far as we are able to discern that activity. This process of unification results in a complexification of the material pole of created being, which in turn intensifies the spiritual pole of created being, the pole of consciousness. Thus far it appears as if matter and spirit simply work in tandem spiritualizing the universe—matter giving birth to spirit and spirit reacting on matter to make it ever more prolific. However, matter and spirit also exist in a relationship of tension, inasmuch as matter is fundamentally a tendency towards that initial multiplicity out of which creation has emerged, whereas spirit is driving ever onwards and upwards away from multiplicity. To the extent that matter is caught up in the dynamics of spirit it ascends, and to the extent that spirit is caught up in the dynamics of matter it descends. The story of creation is the story of a struggle between two directional vectors of the evolutionary movement—matter and spirit. But in the end, the victory is promised to spirit and life. We may schematize Teilhard's understanding, then, as follows: beginning from unity (the Trinity), we pass to pure multiplicity, and then to increasingly unified states of multiplicity. Two movements of created reality are evident: spatially speaking, one movement (spirit) is ascending upwards, the other (matter) is descending downwards; temporally speaking, one movement (spirit) is advancing forwards into the future, the other (matter) is regressing backwards into the past. Teilhard combines both the spatial and the temporal directions by speaking of spirit as "the direction of movement upwards and forwards," and of matter as "the direction of movement downwards and backwards." Such a view is clearly founded upon the primacy of spirit over matter, the future over the past, and unity over multiplicity. We may also say that evolution is basically a struggle between spirit and matter, the future and the past, unity and multiplicity, life and death, being and non-being, good and evil. We thus arrive at a picture of creation as an ascending movement of unification making its way forwards against the tendencies and forces of a descending movement of decomposition seeking to fragment created reality into multiplicity. The question immediately presents itself: whence these negative tendencies and forces? The problem of evil in all its vexing acuity! The movement of evolution is caught within two contrary fields of force—one dominated by a pole of unity up ahead, the other dominated by a pole of multiplicity back behind. Nothing could sound, on first hearing, more Manichaean. Why a pole of multiplicity exercising influence over creation? To what extent is God responsible for the evil in his own good creation? To these questions Teilhard essayed a variety of answers, to which we must now turn.

Involution

Particularly in his earlier writings, Teilhard showed a willingness to entertain at least the possibility that a phase of involution had preceded the presently observable phase of evolution. A few texts will serve to indicate what Teilhard means by involution. In a letter to his cousin in December of 1918, Teilhard, commenting on a work of Schuré's he was reading at the time, says:

I have also come to feel that the problem of creation, looked at not in its present (evolutive) phase but in its initial (involutive) phase, is taking on increasing importance in my mind. What is the origin of that inferior level of multiplicity? What "need" is filled by the fundamental fragmentation of being—driven from its source before returning to it? Until this problem is more or less coherently cleared up, one cannot, I think, understand the worth of souls and the value of the incarnation.[1]

In the following month another reference to involution appears:

Although pagan mythologies are shot through with confused but nonetheless illuminating suggestions regarding the involution of souls, divine incarnations, the association of evil and being, one is somewhat amazed to find that the usual Christian presentation of the origins and vicissitudes of the world are so incredibly artificial, not to say infantile.[2]

In the spring of that same year this concern with an involutive phase of the universe's history comes to focus in an attempt to reinterpret the notion of original sin:

The spectacle of such a suffering and evil multiplicity, abandoned by the world like so much refuse, serves to explain without difficulty the persistency of the notion that the original multiplicity of the cosmos is the trace of some pre-cosmic fall through which spirit was fragmented. According to such a hypothesis, the laborious process of *evolution* which we ourselves experience would then constitute an expiatory phase following upon an original phase of culpable *involution*.

There is surely a profound analogy (a revelatory one perhaps?) between these rather bizarre beliefs and the dogma of original sin. . . . From the Christian point of view, the tendency to plurality, indissolubly bound up with all our efforts towards unification and hence playing the role of a sort of continual temptation, represents in effect a real *inclination*, an evil *bent*, the *memory* of some former state (=*fomes peccati*). And this positive tendency towards retrogression is further complicated by the equally positive role played by the Powers of Darkness.

Ex dogmate, evil matter, which is fundamentally an evil *direction* (the direction of disintegration) in matter, seems to have finally become *embodied* in a group of *habitus* and fallen monads, who constitute, in direct opposition to God, a *real pole* of attraction towards dissociation.[3]

It is with the problem of original sin that the notion of involution will by and large remain connected in the succeeding years. In 1922 Teilhard takes up the theme again:

It would be possible to represent Adam and Eve, before the Fall, as possessing a humanity which was more spiritual than ours is. Owing to an act of infidelity analogous to that of the angels, this pre-humanity would have become less spiritual and hence more material. It is precisely this process of materialization which would have given rise to that painful multiplicity out of which consciousness is presently emerging from all sides albeit with great difficulty. Consequently, we would have to take into consideration not one but two phases in the total cycle of our universe: first, a phase of involution into matter (a "descending" dispersion of a centrifugal kind emanating from the first Adam), which finally results in the formation of the present world; secondly, a phase of evolution in the direction of spirit (concentration of a centripetal kind in the second Adam) directed towards the completion of the new earth.

Scientifically speaking, we discover only the perspectives of the second phase (inasmuch as scientific analysis can only reconstruct the evolutionary past); and we are able to carry these perspectives back, by means of our tools of analysis, almost indefinitely in the direction of an increasingly dissociated multiplicity. However, no means now available to us will ever enable us to discover Adam or Eden since both Adam and Eden belong to a different perspective.[4]

Teilhard characterizes this approach, which "is particularly compatible with a metaphysics of an idealist cast," as being somewhat "fantastic."[5]

In 1924, however, he returns to the same hypothesis:

At the beginning of the sensible world, there was multiplicity; and this block of indissoluble multiplicity had already begun its ascent towards spirit due to the attraction of the cosmic Christ who was coming to birth within it.

However, this ascension involved a slow and painful process because there was already something inherently evil about multiplicity.

What is the origin of this primordial taint in the universe? Why do we feel compelled to identify in some way evil and matter, evil and determinism, evil and plurality? Could it be simply because the inferior zones of the universe and of union represent, relative to our own soul, a terrain long since transcended and hence now forbidden to us—where we would inevitably corrupt ourselves if we decided to return? Is it not more likely, on the other hand, as the Bible itself seems to suggest in a rather formal way, that the original multiplicity came to birth as the result of the dissociation of a being already unified (the first Adam)? If such were the case, then in the present period the world would not so much be ascending as reascending towards Christ (the second Adam)....

In which case, before the present phase of evolution (of spirit out of matter) we would have to postulate a phase of involution (of spirit into matter). This phase of involution would obviously be irretrievable experimentally inasmuch as it would have developed in a direction other than that of the real.[6]

Some years later, in 1947, Teilhard again takes up the notion of involution in discussing possible representations of the meaning of original sin:

If one is seeking to give expression to a doctrine of original sin of a pan-cosmic character, the first line of approach which has to be taken into consideration is that attempted many centuries ago by the Alexandrian school. This line of approach offers the following process as an explanation of the Fall and its consequences: a) the instantaneous creation of a human creature (humanity) perfect in every respect (the first Adam), whom it would be quite futile to attempt to describe in detail or to count numerically as we shall see in a moment. This constitutes the Edenic phase. b) An act of disobedience of some kind. c) A Fall into multiplicity (that is a Fall giving rise to multiplicity). This constitutes the *pre-cosmic phase of involution*. d) A redemptive ascent by means of a progressive reorganization and reunification towards and in the second Adam. This constitutes the cosmic, historical phase of evolution.

This particular scheme satisfies the general conditions required both by the nature of the world and by christology (as we have already seen) for the adequate solution of the problem of the Fall. Since we ourselves are caught up in the cone of cosmic "ascent," we are therefore quite incapable of perceiving the way which led to our descent and hence we look at the world in terms of an evolution from multiplicity. In the perspective of such an evolution there is really no place for Eden or its inhabitants since we see death as being present everywhere from the very beginning. However, such a perspective does make the redemptive work of Christ truly coextensive with the entire world.

Consequently, the solution is seen to be viable. Nonetheless, for several reasons I am not completely happy with it. First of all, it is obvious that the extra-cosmic part of this little drama sounds rather gratuitous in its assumptions and quite fantastic in its conception. We are clearly moving at this point in a world created solely by the imagination. What is still more important, however, the *instantaneous* creation of the first Adam seems to me to involve a type of operation which is absolutely unintelligible, unless of course we assume that the word "instantaneous" is being used merely to cover up the absence of any effort at explanation. Finally, given the hypothesis of a *unique* and *perfect* individual who is put to the test but a single time, the probability of a Fall actually occurring is so minimal that the Creator is made to appear to be the victim of simply a bit of bad luck when the Fall does occur.[7]

Again in 1953 Teilhard takes up the theme of involution in a discussion of original sin. Having indicated that "there exists an essential connection between evil and the evolutionary process," he goes on to say that "two attitudes or interpretations of the biblical data are possible." It is the first of these two possible interpretations which concerns us here:

According to the one theory (what we may call the Neoplatonic, if not the Manichaean, attitude), multiplicity, the stuff of creation, results from the culpable pulverization of some primordial unity. What this means is that the process of evolution in which we ourselves are involved, represents not so much an ascent as a return to the heights, following upon a Fall (or involution) into matter. And we find that in such a view the sin of Adam is amplified in such a way as to encompass the whole cosmos: an original sin which would have given rise to the present cosmos as the result of some pre- or extra-cosmic catastrophe (that is an original sin whose existence we can deduce from an inspection of the present state of the world but which, historically speaking, is capable neither of being discovered nor verified inasmuch as the whole of history has developed in a way both posterior and exterior to this event). Clearly, a very ingenious solution to the problem.[8]

Teilhard, after setting out his own interpretation of original sin, goes on to reject this first hypothesis with a vehemence which was not evident in our previous citations:

Let us not fool ourselves: what truly endangers the future of Christianity at this moment is the false, insidious, and obscurantist sentiment that the process of cosmogenesis (evolution) in which we are involved is not genetically "pure," —but rather that it represents (whatever the euphemisms employed to make the point) in the last analysis merely an effort to glue everything back together again. Christianity will only recoup its power to influence the world when it finally rejects the last residual traces of Manichaeism and Platonism in its teaching and sets itself to the task of rethinking the doctrine of original sin in terms of progress rather than of a Fall. Original sin does not represent some kind of primordial downgrading of being which in turn necessitates a corresponding movement of ascent by way of evolution; rather, original sin is nothing more than a by-product of evolution.[9]

We shall see later what Teilhard means by speaking of original sin as a "by-product of evolution."

From the texts we have cited, it is clear that Teilhard's own personal attitude towards an involutionary interpretation of original sin went through a discernible process of evolution itself. In the early essays he shows himself sympathetic, indeed inclined, towards such a theory. Later, he begins to marshall arguments against it and, finally, he ends up by rejecting it altogether as endangering the interpretation of evolution and the future effectiveness of Christianity because of what he sees as a subterranean attachment to this theory on the part of Christian theology.

Before attempting to assess the relationship of the theory of an involutionary Fall to Teilhard's overall system, we will first of all have to determine with more precision what Teilhard had in mind when he used the term involution. Did he think of spirit entering into matter for the first time through the Fall or did he think of spirit descending further into matter through the Fall? It is important that we make a choice between these two options because they lead to rather different valuations of matter. In the first case, spirit is not intrinsically related to matter but becomes related to it only through a Fall. Thus matter is a form of punishment for spirit's sin, and spirit's salvation consists in breaking free of matters' thralldom. In the second case, spirit and matter are intrinsically related to one another, and spirit's salvation does not exclude that of matter; rather, the salvation of both of them are intimately linked together.

In the first case, spirit is good to begin with and then becomes ambiguous through a Fall, while matter is inherently evil. In the second case, both spirit and matter are originally good and they both subsequently become ambiguous; neither is inherently evil. The term "ambiguous" is used here to indicate the fact that spirit in the first case and spirit and matter in the second case are able to move in alternative directions even if their inclination, owing to the Fall, is towards the direction of further materialization and dissociation. By "ambiguous," in short, we mean simply that the possibility of a redemptive return to unity exists. This is not true of matter in the first case. These two options are classical alternatives and serve to illustrate clearly the problem with which we are confronted.

Is it possible to determine, then, what Teilhard actually had in mind when he spoke of an involutionary Fall? We may profitably begin with some observations pertinent to our problem made by Bruno de Solages. Having mentioned that Teilhard had proposed two different representations of the Fall, de Solages continues:

> The first of these representations Teilhard owed to his friend Father Pierre Charles. It derived from the Greek patristic tradition. The first man had been created as a spirit and, owing to a fault, fell into matter; this materialization then engendered multiplicity. This whole phase of the universe would be extra-historical. In terms of our experience the universe begins with the reascent of multiplicity.[10]

Now this text would serve to settle the matter if it could be assumed that (1) the Greek patristic representation of the Fall being championed by Pierre Charles had dominated Teilhard's understanding of the question from the beginning;[11] and (2) that the Greek patristic tradition had the same understanding of matter as evil which we have already described. The second of these two assumptions is clearly not tenable, since the Greek Fathers, however much they may have been inspired by various forms of Platonism, were not Manichaeans. The first of these two assumptions has to be tested against the textual evidence.

In the first place, it is not clear that Teilhard simply followed the outline of the Greek patristic representation of the Fall made by de Solages, and presumably espoused by Charles, even in the one essay where Charles' influence is acknowledged. On the contrary, it is noteworthy that Teilhard says that it would be "quite futile to attempt to describe in detail or to count numerically" the first Adam (or Adams).[12] He refuses to take a stand one way or the other on whether or not "Adam" was a pure spirit. The reason for this is that Teilhard feels that "the *instantaneous* creation of the first Adam seems to me to involve a type of operation which is absolutely unintelligible, unless of course we assume that the word "instantaneous" is being used merely to cover up the absence of any effort at explanation."[13] This statement rather clearly indicates that Teilhard cannot conceive of man being created apart from an evolutionary movement. It would also seem to indicate that Teilhard cannot really conceive of man as a pure spirit. We may just note before leaving this essay that Teilhard characterizes this position as Alexandrian,[14] probably in deference to Charles. This point is important because Teilhard does not always use the same label to designate this representation of the Fall.

In 1924, for example, Teilhard says that this representation is biblical.[15] However, in 1953, he characterizes the approach as "Neo-platonic, if not Manichaean."[16] These various designations very likely serve to mark the steps in the evolution of Teilhard's own attitude to the problem of an involuntary Fall. During the early period, when Teilhard was rather well disposed towards this theory, he designates it as biblical. In 1947, when he has already become somewhat disenchanted with the notion, Teilhard describes it as Alexandrian owing to the influence of Pierre Charles. In 1953, when we find the most outspoken rejection of the theory, Teilhard brands it as Neoplatonic if not Manichaean. On the basis of this rather skimpy evidence, we may at least make the following suggestion. Teilhard originally attempted to understand the involutionary Fall in terms of the biblical narrative, and hence thought of Adam and Eve as being in a more spiritual state before the Fall and a more material one after it. Therefore, there is no question at this point of a descent of pure spirit into matter for the first time. This interpretation seems to be confirmed by the following text written in 1922:

It would be possible to represent Adam and Eve, before the Fall, as possessing a humanity which is more spiritual than ours is. Owing to an act of infidelity analogous to that of the angels, this pre-humanity would have become less spiritual, and hence more material . . .[17]

Now when Teilhard through his contact with Pierre Charles became familiar, undoubtedly in a rather rudimentary way, with the Greek patristic understanding of the Fall, he saw that the original Adam was conceived of as having been a pure spirit. He apparently does not wish to accept this viewpoint wholeheartedly and so he refuses to say what the first Adam was like. And since the Fall is still being presented within the context of a basically Christian, if Platonically influenced, understanding of matter, Teilhard sees no great difficulty. However, by 1953 Teilhard has drawn out the consequences of this viewpoint and he sees the Manichaean implications in it. Now he does not give this as his reason for rejecting the theory but it likely colored the rather strong way in which he does reject it.

On the basis of what is admittedly only a tentative hypothesis respecting the development of Teilhard's attitude to and understanding of the theory of an involutionary Fall, we may hazard the assertion that Teilhard in his early period conceived of the involutionary Fall as a further descent into matter rather than as an initial descent into matter. In other words, the Fall gave a negative directionality to matter, a directionality determined by man's freedom, a directionality which it did not have before man's Fall. Before the Fall the directionality of matter is identical with the directionality of spirit. However, through the Fall both become ambiguous, but with a decided tendency towards multiplicity. However, this directionality is reversible if man's freedom can be redeemed from its sin. The direction of both matter and spirit, as determined by man's sin, has, in short, to be inverted by the redemptive activity of Christ.

While Teilhard did not apparently spell out for himself all these implications of the theory of an involutionary Fall, he did sense that this theory served to explain the negative directionality and inclination towards multiplicity observable in matter on the basis of a pre-cosmic and hence unverifiable Fall. The theory of an involutionary Fall is thus seen to cohere with at least this aspect of Teilhard's system and perhaps this serves to explain why Teilhard was initially attracted to it. However, it coheres so poorly with other aspects of Teilhard's system that one is still puzzled in the end by Teilhard's interest in this theory over so long a period of time. We should now like to show the conflict between this theory and Teilhard's overall system in the context of his second alternative representation of the Fall.

Teilhard's Own Solution
to the Problem of Original Sin

Teilhard's own solution to the problem of original sin has been treated in some detail by other commentators,[18] but the importance of the topic, as well as the diversity of opinion engendered by it among the commentators, warrant a reasonably thorough exposition of it here.

We have already seen that Teilhard showed some concern with the problem of original sin during the First World War period,[19] particularly in relation to the theory of an involutionary Fall. However, it is in 1920 that we begin to note a marked increase of interest in the question. At the beginning of that year Teilhard remarks that *"in order that Christ be truly universal,* it is essential that the redemption, and hence the Fall as well, extend to the entire universe."[20] During the summer of the same year he devotes a whole essay to an elaboration of this statement. In order to establish the universality of original sin as a basis for a universal redemption, Teilhard fixes upon the relationship between sin and death discussed by Paul in Romans 5, 12:

Long before man appeared on the earth, there was death. And even in the immensities of extra-terrestrial space, far from any moral influence from earth, there was also death. Now St. Paul is absolutely explicit on this point: *"Per peccatum mors."* (Original) sin is not intended to explain merely human suffering and human mortality. For St. Paul, it serves to explain all suffering. It is the solution to the problem of evil.[21]

Teilhard then goes on to explain himself in greater detail:

Original sin, taken in a generalized sense, is not a specifically terrestrial malady nor is it linked to human generation. Rather, it simply symbolizes the inevitable hazard of evil (*necesse est ut eveniant scandala*) attaching to the existence of all participated being. No matter where being *in fieri* is found, suffering and moral fault immediately make their appearance as a sort of shadow, not only as a result of the tendency of creatures to laziness and egoism, but also (which is even more troubling) as the unavoidable accompaniment of all the creatures' efforts towards progress. Original sin is the essential reaction of the finite to the creative act. Inevitably then, it makes its way into the creation as the result of the very act of creation itself. It is in fact the inverted form of all creation. By the very fact that God creates, he becomes involved in a struggle against evil, and therefore, in one way or another, he becomes involved in a work of redemption.[22]

How does original sin as a specifically human phenomenon fit into this overall picture?

The properly human Fall is nothing other than the actuation (more or less collective and perennial) within our own race of this "*forma peccati*" which had been infused, long before our appearance, into the universe from the lowest zones of matter right up to the angelic spheres. There is not, strictly speaking, a first Adam. Beneath this name lies hidden a universal and unalterable law of reversion and perversion, —the price of our progress.[23]

Leaving aside the rather strange exegesis of Paul which this argument leans upon for support, we see that Teilhard is trying to combine together under the rubric of original sin both physical and moral evil. Now, if we grant that the traditional understanding of original sin also tried to connect the original sin of man with evil in the universe as a whole, then it becomes clear that what Teilhard is attempting is not *ipso facto* illegitimate. The difference between the two positions lies in the fact that they approach the relationship of physical and moral evil from opposite directions. The traditional position starts from a good universe into which physical evil is subsequently introduced by man's sin, whereas Teilhard starts with the inevitable presence of physical evil in an evolving universe and subsequently arrives at moral evil in man, which he considers to be a new and also inevitable modality of the evil which preceded man's appearance.

In 1922, Teilhard returns to the same basic explanation but with particular attention to original sin as a human phenomenon:

Original sin expresses, translates, personifies, in terms of an instantaneous and localized act, the universal and perennial law of moral fault which is in humanity in virtue of its situation of being "*in fieri*." One could perhaps say that because the creative act (by definition) causes being to ascend to God from the frontiers of non-being (that is from the depths of multiplicity, hence from the depths of matter), all creation involves, as its risk and shadow, some failing, that is it is inevitably matched by some kind of redemption. The drama acted out in Eden would be in this conception equivalent to the drama acted out by all men throughout history, but crystallized in the form of a profoundly expressive symbol of the actual reality. Adam and Eve are the images of humanity on its way to God. The beatitude of the terrestrial paradise represents the salvation which is constantly being offered to all, but which is refused by many...[24]

In 1939 Teilhard again returns to the idea of original sin in man as a special modality of the evil everywhere present from the beginning:

I have no objection to admitting that the evil inherent in the world in virtue of its mode of creation could be regarded as being in a particular way individualized on earth at the moment of the appearance of responsible human "selves." This would constitute, in the *strict sense*, what the theologians call "original sin." From another point of view, one might just ask if the true human sin would not be that committed by man once he has attained, much later in history, to a sort of plenitude of consciousness and responsibility.[25]

This distinction is brought out still more clearly in 1942: "Original sin considered in terms of its cosmic foundation (if not in terms of its historical actuation in the first humans) tends to merge with the very mechanism of creation, where it represents the activity of the negative forces of 'counter-evolution.' "[26] From these texts it is clear that Teilhard, as we have said earlier, wishes original sin in its properly human phase to be understood as a modality, or what he calls an "actuation," of original sin in its cosmic phase. Moral evil is a modality of evil in general, and it cannot be construed as the cause of physical evil however much it may serve to aggravate it. We have already seen that Teilhard feels compelled to argue in this fashion because of the evolutionary context in which he thinks. In terms of the static cosmology of the Bible, there is really no other way open to conceive the relationship between moral and physical evil than in terms of cause and effect. For Teilhard, on the other hand, there can be no causal relation between them in either direction since both moral and physical evil result from the same general situation—the imperfect state of an evolving universe emerging from multiplicity into unity. In such a universe evil—both physical and moral—is inevitable; as Teilhard loves to repeat: *"Necesse est ut eveniant scandala"*—it must needs be that scandals come (Mt. 18, 7).[27]

This contention seems to be contradicted, however, by Teilhard's use of the Pauline text, *"per peccatum, mors,"* which does establish an obvious causal link between moral and physical evil. If Teilhard insists on retaining this textual support, he has also to retain the notion of an involutionary Fall which engenders the cosmos. This he cannot do, however, for the simple reason that it negates his whole point that evil is the result of an evolving process. If there is any cause for evil in general, it is God who decided to create by uniting multiplicity. The connection between sin and physical evil established by Paul's text falls completely to the ground. Apparently, Teilhard failed to perceive this. Furthermore, if he wanted to retain the theory of an involutionary Fall, which would not contradict Paul's text, he would be left with humanity as his starting point for evolution which also negates his whole system. Teilhard's rejection of an involutionary Fall as well as Paul's static cosmology, logically forces him to sever any causal link between moral evil and the origin of physical evil. Teilhard cannot legitimately extract himself from this dilemma by making original sin a transhistoric law of the universe as he seeks to do. Sin or moral evil cannot become a causal law of the entire cosmos unless one accepts an involutionary Fall which, as we just observed, will necessitate accepting humanity as the point of departure of evolution which Teilhard cannot do. Strangely enough, Teilhard never adverts to this fact in his discussion of the theory of an involutionary Fall.

The only way Teilhard can possibly retain Paul's text is to rewrite it to read: *"Per malum, mors"*—through evil, death. This is a viable, if unscriptural, formula in that it establishes a link between evil in general and death without making anyone culpable for the evil which leads to death unless it be God who chose to create in an evolutionary form. Following this formula, it would be possible to say that evil will initially assume the modality of physical evil and only after an immense span of time the modality of moral evil. Evil in the second instance becomes properly hominized so to speak. This, as Teilhard admits, is what the theologians mean by "original sin" in the strict sense. What Teilhard fails to see is that there can be no extended sense for the notion of original *sin* as such, for it must be a properly hominized modality of evil. On the other hand, there is no good reason to fault Teilhard for having tried to break the causal nexus between man's sin and death as such, since proponents of a similar view can be found in contemporary Catholic theology.[28] For example, Karl Rahner argues that sin introduces a new modality into human death—an element of darkness—rather than that it causes death itself.[29] It is quite impossible, however, for Teilhard to retain the Pauline formula by cosmicizing it, and there is, moreover, no need for him to do so.

3

What Teilhard has done is to amalgamate together in an illegitimate way the problem of evil in general with the doctrine of original sin in particular. He was likely driven to this by the connection established in the theology with which he was familiar between moral and physical evil, a connection deriving from a static cosmology as he rightly notes. What Teilhard did, then, was to apply to the problem of original sin the very same solution which he arrived at for the problem of evil in general. Such a procedure involves him ultimately in a terminological impasse, since the terminological rubric original sin cannot be applied to the solution of the problem of evil in general *in Teilhard's own system*. He is guilty of a rather radical inconsistency at this point, if our analysis is correct.

However, this is not to say necessarily that there are no valuable elements in his analysis of the problem, even if his proposed solution is of somewhat dubious value as it stands. What should be kept in mind is that Teilhard's concern with the traditional representation of original sin was not solely motivated by the scandal it seemed to present for his scientific world view. In point of fact, Teilhard's concern in this area was primarily theological rather than scientific. It was in order to protect the truly cosmic character of Christ's redemptive function that Teilhard undertook a revision of the doctrine of original sin. Everything he has to say about original sin is subordinated to and derived from this overarching motivation. Teilhard is afraid that if original sin is confined to man and if redemption is understood in relationship to such a notion of original sin, then Christ will become the local god of but a small portion of the universe. If the whole cosmos is in a state of evolutionary flux and if evil is, as a result, everywhere present in the cosmos, then Christ must be made to be the redeemer of the total cosmos from evil—he must become the God of evolution *tout court*. Modern man, according to Teilhard, can no longer worship a tribal god, even if the tribe over which he exercises dominion be as vast as the whole of humanity on this planet.

If the entire cosmos is evolutionary in character and if evil is an inevitable concomitant of the evolutionary process (the modality of creation being evolutionary as far as we are able to tell), the movement of evolution must involve not only a creative activity on God's part, but also at the same time a redemptive activity.

The creative process which involves a unification of multiplicity is also a redemptive process because unification involves a struggle against the forces of dispersion, the forces of evil. Hence creation and redemption are coextensive with the total space-time continuum. More than this, the incarnation, in the general sense of an immersion of God in the evolutionary process, is likewise coextensive with the total space-time continuum. This emphasis is already evident in 1918:

While creation, incarnation, and redemption each mark a further level of gratuity in the divine operation, is it not also true that these three acts are indissolubly bound together in the appearance of participated being?[30]

Again in 1922:

Creation, Fall, incarnation, and redemption . . . all four together become coextensive with the duration and the totality of the world; they constitute, in some sense, the really distinct but nonetheless physically connected aspects of one and the same divine operation.[31]

And in 1944:

Christianity, influenced by the conquests of modern thought, will finally become aware of the fact that the three fundamental personalistic mysteries upon which it rests are in reality simply three aspects of one and the same process (christogenesis), depending on whether one looks at it from the point of view of its principal moving power (creation), or its unifying mechanism (incarnation), or its elevating effort (redemption) . . .[32]

And finally, in 1947:

Creation, incarnation, and redemption appear now as simply complementary aspects of one and the same process: creation (because it is a unifying process) necessitating a certain immersion of the creator in his work, and at the same time a certain redemptive compensation (because such a process of necessity generates evil as its secondary statistical effect).[33]

Again, Teilhard seems to shy away from historicizing any of his key concepts in favor of a position which cosmicizes them all. Virtually every important element in the cosmic process is coextensive with the whole. This is true of consciousness, freedom, spirit, life, love, creation, incarnation, and redemption. Is it, then, that for Teilhard there is truly *"nihil novum sub sole"*?

Typology in Teilhard

In order to answer this question, which is quite crucial to a proper understanding of Teilhard's thought, it is first of all imperative that one begin with a clear notion of Teilhard's methodological key for interpreting history. Teilhard reads history (taken in the broad sense) typologically. What this means is that Teilhard understands every phase of history in terms of an overarching paradigmatic pattern applicable to each phase, at least in terms of its basic ingredients. Such a method will allow him to see continuity between all the phases of history because the ingredients are all the same. This is the cosmicizing aspect of his typological method, and it necessitates the postulation of a fundamental coextension of all the basic cosmic elements enumerated above.

This raises the question whether or not Teilhard leaves any room for discontinuity between the various phases of history. We can answer this question affirmatively and without hesitation. For example, the consciousness present at the pre-life phase of history is not the same as the consciousness present at the human phase of history, and this is equally true of life, freedom, spirit, love, and so forth. The one is rudimentary and experimentally indiscernible, while the other is highly developed and only too evident. The term "consciousness" applies with full force to man, and can only be applied to pre-life in an attenuated or analogical sense. This element of discontinuity in Teilhard's system betrays its ontological depth and its capacity for distinguishing ontological levels. However, for the term "ontological" we may substitute here the term "historical" with the following result: the postulation of discontinuity constitutes the historicizing aspect of Teilhard's typological method, and it necessitates a fundamental, irreducible distinction between the phases of history. A typological method seeks basically to handle both continuity and discontinuity within history, to pinpoint the similarity within the difference as well as the difference within the similarity. This Teilhard consistently seeks to do.

These reflections can be drawn together into an image which translates Teilhard's vision of history into concrete terms. A typological interpretation of history, assuming that it has ontological depth, is explicable in terms of the geometrical model of a spiral[34] rather than a circle or a straight line, although it incorporates the basic impulse of both of these. The circle translates a cyclical interpretation of history whose fundamental motif is recurrence, whereas a straight line translates a linear interpretation of history whose fundamental motif is novelty. The spiral, on the other hand, translates history in terms of ascending plateaus, in which patterns recur together with an element of novelty. On each plateau one finds the same basic drama being enacted, but with a difference of ontological depth. In this way, each preceding plateau provides an outline of what follows, even if in a very real sense the next level is unpredictable in detail because of the discontinuity involved. As the spiral ascends, the drama becomes richer because the elements which were already present become more clearly manifest because of their more refined ontological articulation. Without such a typological method of interpretation it is difficult to see how Teilhard could find in the past valuable, even crucial, evidence for assessing the present and most particularly the future. And his conviction that the pattern will go on repeating itself into the future rests upon the fact that the ingredients in his pattern include not only consciousness, freedom, love, spirit, and life, but also, and what is more important, creation, incarnation, and redemption. It is the divine activity which gives him his indispensable guarantee of final success, and it is this which gives substance to his optimism.

While it is true that Teilhard nowhere explicitly offers us typology as his methodological tool of explanation, he does think of the law of complexity-consciousness as such a key, and it is significant that he calls it "a law of recurrence."[35] However, the law of complexity-consciousness as such cannot offer any guarantee of continuing recurrence precisely because it cannot, as a phenomenologically derived datum, include the dimension of divine activity. The law of complexity-consciousness as a law of recurrence can open up the hope of continued recurrence into the future, but it cannot guarantee its being well-founded. In a sense, then, the analysis of the movement of evolution which led ultimately to the formulation of the law of complexity-consciousness constitutes the analysis of a problematic, the problematic of the future. Such an analysis raises a question about our possibilities for the future; it serves to engender a hope. The introduction of the divine activity as creative and redemptive seeks to answer that question, and to show that such a hope is not illusory.

If our argument respecting the existence of at least an implicit typological method in Teilhard's approach to history has any validity at all, then it is reasonable to ask whence Teilhard derived his basic paradigm for understanding the meaning of history. Did he begin with an analysis of the level of pre-life and work from a paradigm discovered there to all the succeeding levels? This seems unlikely even in principle since, as we saw previously, Teilhard is not terribly concerned with origins and initial manifestations, feeling that they represent the most obscure aspect of any process. It is only as the process unfolds that intelligibility emerges—the pattern becomes clear only after an immense span of time. Should we not rather suspect that Teilhard began initially with the human phenomenon (the historical aspect of his typological method) and proceeded from there to apply the human paradigm to the whole (the cosmicizing aspect of his typological method)? It is man who provides the key of interpretation, and the great themes of the human drama are the great themes of the cosmic drama. The same pattern is applicable to the total cosmos, but it is only in and with man that the pattern finds perfectly manifest exemplification.

We have already suggested that this is true with respect to Teilhard's understanding of the matter/spirit relationship, and we would now like to suggest that it is also true of Teilhard's understanding of original sin. It is initially obvious that Teilhard started with a notion of original sin which applied to man; in fact, it was this very fact that caused him to cast about for a new representation of the dogma of original sin inasmuch as he felt that a localized original sin necessitated a localized redemption and hence destroyed the cosmic character of Christ. It is not so much that Teilhard intended to depersonalize original sin as that he tried to give it a cosmic extension by amalgamating it with the broader question of the problem of evil in general. As a result, the question of original sin becomes a question of the problem of physical as well as moral evil. What is confusing is that Teilhard retains the term "original sin" to cover both these aspects of the problem of evil, whereas the notion of sin can only refer to moral evil alone.

Furthermore, Teilhard's exegesis of Romans 5, 12 is clearly specious, even if in the process Teilhard does raise a quite tantalizing question about the traditional notion that physical evil results from the moral evil of the first parents. Sin does not introduce physical evil into the world for the first time, it aggravates the physical evil that is already there. Now, if we leave aside terminological and exegetical inadequacies, what do we come up with? Following our typological methodology, we may say that evil, which for Teilhard is fundamentally disunity and multiplicity resulting in suffering and death, is coextensive with the total space-time continuum (the cosmicizing aspect of typology), although it is modalized in a particular way in man (the historicizing aspect of typology). In other words, the paradigmatic pattern of evil as multiplicity is to be found in man, but it can be extrapolated into the past so as to take on cosmic dimensions. There is a similarity between physical and moral evil, and there is also a considerable difference between them. A typological method has to account for both these aspects, and it seems that Teilhard does this by considering them different modalities of evil in general.

Now, as we have seen, Teilhard inconsistently tries to retain the causal nexus by seeking support in Romans 5, 12 for his own attempt to transhistoricize original sin into a cosmic law. Possibly, Teilhard, more or less unconsciously, felt compelled to retain the rubric original sin to cover what in fact could not be covered by such a notion because of his quite conscious attempt to extend the redemptive function of Christ so as to encompass the whole cosmos. Since redemption and original sin have traditionally been paired, Teilhard may have believed that he had to keep to the traditional categories in order to win a hearing among theologians for his position. If the terms "original sin" and "redemption" are going to be retained in such an unusual context, then they have to be understood in a carefully nuanced analogical sense, which Teilhard does not do. In line with the typological methodology outlined above, we may retain the term "redemption," but the term "original sin" hardly seems viable and should in fact be reserved only for evil in its properly hominized form. These corrective suggestions do not violate Teilhard's deepest intentions; on the contrary, they serve rather to rectify the illogical inconsistency in his actual argumentation.

Monogenism/Polygenism

It should be noted further that Teilhard breaks with the traditional representation of original sin in two other ways significant for an appreciation of his position on this question. First of all, Teilhard is never very interested in origins (as we have seen), and hence it would be more likely for him to try to understand the nature of sin from the end rather than the beginning. We have already quoted one text to indicate this.[36] Teilhard prefers to read history in terms of Christ rather than in terms of Adam. He suspects the traditional representation of original sin of being so concerned with origins and the after-effects of Adam's sin at the beginning that it cannot do justice to the continuous creative and redemptive work of Christ. The traditional representation lends itself all too readily to pessimism in Teilhard's mind, and he is concerned to offset this tendency in his own position. Secondly, Teilhard contested the monogenistic underpinnings of the dogma of original sin,[37] and hence it was impossible for him to think of Adam as an individual in the first place. He knows only of a group of first parents whose sins he is willing to concede may well have been decisive even if they were committed with minimal consciousness. At the moment, there appears to be no good reason to fault Teilhard for holding a polygenistic hypothesis in that the monogenism/polygenism debate may legitimately be considered to be viable since it focuses on a question which is increasingly admitted to be an open one.[38]

Summary

We are now in a position to summarize the results of our investigation into Teilhard's treatment of original sin. Teilhard generally presented two alternative representations of the Fall. The first representation posits a pre-cosmic Fall on the part of man from a state of unity into a state of multiplicity. In his initial attempts to work out this theory. Teilhard probably did little more than transpose the Genesis narrative from an "historical" setting to a transhistorical one in order to avoid the difficulty of having to consider Adam as one link in a chain. For Teilhard felt that if Adam were understood in such a serial fashion, the universality of sin and hence of redemption would be destroyed. Original sin and its concomitant effect death must be present from the very beginning, in Teilhard's mind, and thus the notion of a pre-cosmic Fall of a transhistoric kind would serve to make original sin and death ubiquitously present in history. Such a view of the Fall would also serve to account for the negative directionality of matter (which originally was good), and explain the origin of the world in multiplicity (even if it is by no means clear how such a multiplicity as Teilhard conceived of as being present at the beginning of the world could have been engendered through a Fall). If this theory solves certain of Teilhard's problems and coheres with certain aspects of his system, it ultimately creates more difficulties than it solves and also stands in radical contradiction to Teilhard's overall evolutionary system, principally because it begins with man, who can hardly be eliminated after the Fall occurs.

We also explored Teilhard's own theory[39] of the Fall in the context of an evolutionary world view. Again, Teilhard tries to make original sin coextensive with the whole course of evolution, but since he logically cannot start with man and his freedom in this second alternative representation, he reaches at least a terminological impasse through his amalgamation of physical and moral evil under the single term "original sin." We suggested that Teilhard, if he had wished to be consistent, should have cleanly broken the causal link between moral and physical evil established by the traditional understanding of original sin. In terms of Teilhard's own system, physical evil cannot be causally related to moral evil, it can only be aggravated by moral evil since it antedates moral evil. Thus moral evil would become a modality of evil in general, the hominized form of evil. This understanding of moral evil as a modality of evil in general would then be equivalent to original sin, not in the strict sense as Teilhard maintains, but in the only possible sense since the very notion of sin implies freedom and moral responsibility.

By correcting certain terminological and exegetical weaknesses in Teilhard's approach to original sin, we would seem to have present in these reflections the elements for a fruitful rethinking of the notion of original sin, even if there are obvious lacunae in Teilhard's position. In the last analysis, Teilhard's most valuable contribution to the discussion of the problem of evil may well be not his contention that sin, just as evil in general, originates out of statistical necessity, but rather his analysis of the nature of evil as the flight into multiplicity. It is this analysis that we must now turn to in the next chapter. We will focus there on evil as a human phenomenon and try to see how Teilhard understands the nature of original sin in man even though he does not use the term "original sin" in this connection. We hope to be able in this way to indicate that Teilhard does take original sin seriously as a human phenomenon, and that he does not simply depersonalize the notion of sin as seems likely *prima facie* owing to his attempt to amalgamate physical and moral evil together under the rubric original sin.

IV

Love: The Energy of Unification

With this chapter we begin our analysis of the problem of the one and the many as a specifically human problem, as a problem of the socialization of mankind. We will be concerned with Teilhard's efforts to unify the multiplicity which is mankind in such a way as not only to safeguard, but indeed to enhance and perfect person-hood. Consequently, we will be particularly concerned with Teilhard's understanding of the role of love in the evolutionary development of the world as the energy of both unification and personalization. However, only a very special kind of love is able, in Teilhard's mind, to resolve the properly hominized form of the problem of the one and the many—a love capable of unifying the noosphere, a universal form of love transcending all the limitations and ambiguities inherent in forms of love which unify only rela-tively small parts of the noosphere. We will see that according to Teilhard what is needed is a form of love which goes beyond the unifying capacities of sexual love, friendship, and patriotism. But before exploring Teilhard's understanding of a universal love as the solution to the problem of the unification of the hominized many in more detail, we must first see how Teilhard views the multiplicity of mankind in the context of what he calls "the crisis of reflection," a notion which we hope to show constitutes a further elaboration by Teilhard of the doctrine of original sin, the subject of our last chapter.

The Crisis of Reflection

"The appearance of the immortal soul gave rise to a frightening crisis of individuation in the world, that is *a destructive return to multiplicity*, a diminishing, painful, culpable multiplicity."[1] The "step of reflection," as Teilhard frequently calls it, marks the inauguration of a formidable crisis in the movement of evolution, the movement of creation. For, with the appearance of reflection, a new and devastating power of dispersion is let loose in the world; the danger of a final and irreducible multiplicity appears in all its acuity.

It is interesting to note that Teilhard sees this crisis introduced by reflection and hence freedom as both inevitable and culpable. Would it be gratuitous to suggest that this inevitable and culpable flight into multiplicity on the part of man represents Teilhard's most penetrating insight into the notion of original sin? That a link between the crisis of reflection and original sin does in fact exist is suggested in a later essay:

This way of understanding original sin clearly obviates every difficulty of a scientific kind (inasmuch as original sin becomes an integral part of the evolution of the world). On the other hand, this approach does possess the disadvantage of forcing us to do away with an individual first parent called "Adam" and an initial Fall, unless we are willing to consider the "original fault" to have been the moral crisis which very likely accompanied the initial appearance of intelligence in humanity . . .[2]

The crisis of reflection is identical with the human condition. It is both an inevitable consequence of being human, of being born into the world, and a culpable fault as well in that each man, through his own personal egoism and pleasure-seeking, ratifies the innate human tendency to fragment the world into multiple islands of isolated self-aggrandizement. The crisis of reflection occurs inevitably with the initial step of reflection at the beginning of human history, but the crisis grows apace with the growth of consciousness. Again, we see that this thematic parallels in certain respects the thematic attaching to the interpretation of original sin worked out by Teilhard.

If the crisis of reflection at its most fundamental level constitutes a crisis in interpersonal relationships, it also represents a crisis of meaning. This is particularly true at that point in history when man becomes aware of evolution and of his own responsibility for the successful outcome of evolution. When man, through his powers of reflection, evaluates life and tries to seek a meaning for his own life within the context of the totality of life, the whole of life runs a serious risk inasmuch as man may come to the conclusion that life is a scandal, that it has no meaning. As a result of such a conclusion, he may well decide to exploit life for what he can get out of it for himself with the least effort. Even if he concludes that life is worthwhile, he may restrict its meaning to his own personal self-achievement. In either case, every man inevitably tends to center the world on himself and thus the whole movement of life is threatened by a retrogressive movement of individualism, a movement towards a hominized form of that initial multiplicity which the entire process of evolution has been striving to overcome through unification. In a very real sense, all creation, as a process involving the unification of the multiple, begins anew with the appearance of man who constitutes a new and even more dangerous form of multiplicity precisely because he is able to refuse unification by retiring into himself and thus relating to the world in a purely egocentric fashion.

The problem of meaning serves to aggravate further that endemic and mysterious tendency of human beings to withdraw into themselves in egoism and pleasure-seeking, a tendency which has existed from the very beginning. The tendency to individualism represents the hominized form of that tendency to multiplicity which Teilhard notes as the directional characteristic of matter. But whereas with matter this tendency is simply inevitable, with man it also becomes culpable. This suggests that the tendency to multiplicity in man is a reversible trend, since it arises in part at least from freedom of choice. If matter can escape to some extent from its own innate tendency to dispersion through the uniting activity of spirit, man can also escape from his own innate tendency to individualism through union with others, through the power of love. It will be the work of love to unite what is separated, but love will constantly have to struggle against the forces of dispersion—egoism, pleasure-seeking, hate—which seek to widen further an already existing gulf of separation. The struggle between love and individualism is similar, then, to the struggle being waged between life and entropy; in fact, it represents the hominized form of that struggle.

If the analogy between the unification of matter and the unification of mankind has any validity, it inevitably raises a further question. Granted that the unification of matter involves a creative as well as a redemptive activity on the part of God, since matter is incapable of unifying itself or redeeming itself from its own tendency to multiplicity, then it may be asked if the unification of mankind does not also involve a creative as well as a redemptive activity on the part of God. Can the trend towards multiplicity evident with the step of reflection and aggravated by the growth of consciousness be reversed simply by an act of human freedom? Is mankind in the last analysis self-uniting or at least could it be self-uniting if it willed to be? To ask this question is already to anticipate on the subject matter of following chapters, and hence we will allow the question to stand until we are in a better position to see how Teilhard sets about answering it. We may just remark at this point that, if our contention that the crisis of reflection thematic is bound up with the problem of original sin is correct, then it seems more than likely that the crisis of reflection problematic will require a redemptive solution. It also indicates that Teilhard does not view spirit as simply a directional vector towards unity. For, owing to original sin or the crisis of reflection, spirit in its hominized form is caught up in the thrust of matter towards multiplicity. Hence, if spirit is to be the unifying principle of the noosphere, its inclination towards dissociation and fragmentation must be inverted just as the inclination of matter towards multiplicity must be inverted by spirit if it is to be complexified so as to become the matrix for the growth of spirit. And again the question of redemption emerges into view.

Love: The Energy of Unification

We have seen that the step of reflection inaugurates a new movement of fragmentation leading to the positing of a new multiplicity. If our suggestion that this thematic translates into other categories an understanding of original sin as a flight into multiplicity is correct, then it is possible to suggest further that this thematic offers an interesting parallel with the early chapters of the Book of

Genesis, particularly the Cain and Abel and Tower of Babylon narratives, which understand sin precisely as a destructive power of dispersion. On the other hand, where the biblical narrative begins with an initial state of unity which is subsequently broken down by the sin of Adam, Teilhard begins with an initial multiplicity which has yet to be unified.

The appearance and multiplication of mankind demands that creation be begun anew in that a new and formidable multiplicity has now to be unified. And if the original multiplicity of creation (that is matter) was not simply a neutral base for unification, but rather possessed an inherent tendency to further multiplicity which had to be inverted through the forces of unification, so too man as the new multiplicity of creation is not simply a neutral base for unification, but rather possesses an inherent tendency to further multiplicity which has to be inverted through the new forces of unification. In other words, a struggle between the forces of dispersion and the forces of unification takes place in both instances. This correspondence between the initial creation (centering on matter) and the new creation (centering on spirit) is not totally unexpected in light of Teilhard's typological method. For, according to the typological method outlined in the last chapter, the ingredients and thematic of the pre-hominized phase of evolution will remain valid during this new phase of evolution, but they will be present with a new ontological depth since they will all appear now in their properly hominized form. And again we may ask if the hominized form of the thematic does not in fact represent the paradigmatic pattern in terms of which the pre-hominized form of the thematic has been worked out.

We have thus far concentrated our attention on spirit and consciousness as fundamental ingredients of the cosmic drama of evolution. We must now see how Teilhard understands love as the ubiquitous energy of unification in the cosmos—the power which is continually overcoming multiplicity, the power of growing synthesis. So central is love to Teilhard's conception of the development of the world that he can say that "the most striking and at the same time the most profoundly accurate way in which to recount the story of universal evolution would undoubtedly be to retrace the evolution of love."[3]

One of Teilhard's very earliest essays, "L'Eternel féminin," is precisely an attempt to depict the history of the evolution of love in a highly poetical, mystical way. He applies to love the text from Proverbs 8, 22, "*ab initio creata sum*," to indicate that love has been present and active from the very beginning, and then goes on to summarize the role which love is to play.

Everything in the universe comes to be through union and fecundity—through the coming together of two elements which seek each other out and which through their union are reborn in the form of a new reality.

God sent me (i.e. love) into the world in order to create unity out of what was at the beginning nothing more than sheer multiplicity.

It is I who join the multiple together—it is the scent of my perfume which draws them freely, indeed passionately, towards oneness.[4]

Even at the atomic level love is at work:

Somewhat like a soul as yet barely awakened but nonetheless indispensable for movement, I (i.e. love) was at work from the very beginning, as a field of attractive force, within what was then little more than an amorphous mass; I made even the atoms, infinitesimal as they are, feel that vague but irrepressible restlessness which arises from the desire to escape from the impotency of solitude; I made them want to enter into relation with something outside of themselves.

It was in this way that I cemented together the very foundations of the universe.[5]

That Teilhard is here thinking of love in an analogical sense is made clear in a later essay.

At the level of pre-life and at the level of the pre-human in general, love, in the strict sense of the word, does not yet exist, because the centers are either not yet centered or are only imperfectly so. However, it still seems appropriate to use the term "love" in this connection. For although love is here present only in its incipient forms, it will gradually evolve under the influence of that mutual affinity which brings the particles together and causes them to remain united throughout the course of their forward movement of convergence.[6]

If it is true that love is already present at the stage of pre-life, it is only with the appearance of life that love begins to take on a more clearly defined form.

With the appearance of life, I began to take form in those especially chosen to exist as my image, gradually taking on more clearly individualized traits.

Indistinct and elusive at first, as if I were hesitating to become concrete within the limitations of some palpable form, I slowly revealed myself in more finely differentiated ways to the extent that souls became more capable of richer, more profound, and more spiritual forms of union.[7]

This whole movement of love within the sphere of the pre-human is summed up in bold strokes by Teilhard in *The Phenomenon of Man*:

Considered in its full biological reality, love—that is to say, the affinity of one thing for another—is not peculiar to man. It is a general property of all life and as such it embraces, in different ways and in varying degrees, all the forms successively adopted by organized matter. In the mammals, so close to ourselves, it is easily recognized in its different modalities: sexual passion, parental instinct, social solidarity, etc. At a further remove, lower down on the tree of life, the analogies are more obscure until they become so faint as to be imperceptible. But it is surely in order at this point to repeat what was said earlier with regard to the "within of things." If there were no internal propensity to unite, even at an unimaginably rudimentary level—indeed at the molecular level itself—it would be physically impossible for love to appear at a higher level, with us, in hominized form. In point of fact, to be certain of its presence in ourselves, we should assume its presence, at least in inchoate form, in everything that is.... Driven by the power of love, the fragmented elements of the world seek each other out so that the world may reach its final goal. This is no mere metaphorical way of speaking and it is certainly not to be ascribed to sheer poetic fancy.[8]

At each stage the forms of love observable at the lower stages are transformed and incorporated into a more complex synthesis; they do not simply disappear. All the forms of love, for example, which Teilhard has enumerated with respect to the mammals are also present in man but in a transformed, elevated state. In other words, there is both continuity and discontinuity.

We have already seen from our previous analysis that with the entry of love into the properly hominized sphere of evolution a crisis arises which threatens to bring the evolutionary process to a halt owing to the inevitable and yet culpable tendency of the individual to turn in on himself, to refuse the gift of himself to others in love. This crisis of individualism due to the emergence of reflection and hominized freedom within cosmogenesis can only be offset by the cultivation or, as Teilhard would say, the activation[9] of a form of love strong enough to counteract the tendency to multiplicity already let loose in the world by the step of reflection. What is needed is a universal form of love which will unite together all the members of the noosphere. Every other form of love, precisely because it is limited in scope, unites only fragments of the noosphere and thus in its own way is at the same time divisive of the whole. This may be illustrated from the example of sexual attraction and its history in evolution.

The Evolution of the Sexual Sense

The role of sex within cosmogenesis, like everything else, undergoes a development. At the animal level sex is exclusively orientated towards reproduction and hence the preservation of the species. This also seems to be the case with man, at least in a general way and for a long period of his development. However, it has gradually become apparent that sex has a role to play also in the process of the spiritual molecularization of the noosphere with a consequent diminution of the reproductive aspect of the sexual function.[10] The evolution of the sexual sense implies a spiritualizing and personalizing of the sexual function.

However, this is only to look at one side of the question: what ought to be. In the concrete order of things, sex is by no means an unambiguous reality. That this is the case becomes clear, first of all, in the fact that sexual attraction constitutes but a limited overcoming of the general repulsion which occurs with the appearance of reflection and which is concretely manifested in the tendency of each individual to close in on himself. Hence in and of itself it cannot produce that unitive energy which planetary molecularization requires and which only a universal love can provide. Secondly, there is a tendency for the couple to reënact at their own level that turning in upon themselves which is visible at the individual level.[11]

Sexual attraction, a limited form of unifying energy in the cosmos, can unfortunately result in simply a new form of "*égoisme à deux*," a new and perhaps more destructive form of individualism. As Teilhard laments:

Leaving to one side, if you wish, every trace of sentimentality and any hint of virtuous scandal, let us look quite objectively, in our role as biologists or engineers, at our brilliantly lighted metropolises at night. There—and everywhere else as well—we will see the earth dissipating its most marvelous power in pure waste. The earth is, as it were, going up in smoke and ashes. How much energy, do you think, is lost in a single night that might have been converted into a new spirit of the earth?[12]

From the context in which this text appears, it is evident that Teilhard has in mind primarily the loss of energy due to uncreative and unenriching sexual relationships. Beneath this text lies an attempt to translate the law of entropy in physical reactions into the context of personal relationships in order to underline the retrogressive and dispersive character of sexual relationships which arise out of egoism and pleasure-seeking. This is one direction, the direction of multiplicity, in which sexual relationships can move, but it is not the only one, as we have seen. Teilhard appreciates the ambiguity of sex as he appreciates the ambiguity of matter. Sex can be a unifying experience, but if it is true to its own inner dynamics, it will unify not only the couple itself, but it will also serve to lead the couple into a broader unity with others. Sexual love as a limited victory over the forces of multiplicity in the noosphere cannot furnish of and by itself the energy necessary to cement the noosphere together into unity, but it can, at its best, provide a point of departure for that universal, disinterested love which is required if evolution is to continue onwards and upwards.

What has been said of sexual love as a limited form of love overcoming multiplicity may with equal validity be applied to other limited forms of love like parental care, friendship, and patriotism. An ingrained ambiguity attaches to each of these, an ambiguity rooted in the person who tends towards a spurious autonomy instead of community. At their best, each of these forms of love may serve as a valid point of departure for a more all-embracing form of love, but often enough these limited forms of love serve only to create new divisions within the noosphere by actualizing the tendency to individualism at a wider level of community. What is needed is not only a love capable of uniting individuals together into basic community patterns, but rather a love capable of uniting individuals and their communities into a global community. As Teilhard put it in 1926 in a letter to his cousin:

What I want to do, in short, is to express the psychology—the mixed feelings of pride, hope, disappointment, expectation—of the man who sees himself no longer as a Frenchman or a Chinaman but as a *terrestrial*. The further I go the more determined I become to live above political and national prejudices of any sort, and to say openly what I think without taking any notice of what others say or have said. I believe that the time has come when, if men are ever to achieve a common understanding, they must do so at a point which will be reached only by breaking, reversing or reframing a mass of conventions and prejudices that enclose us in a dead outer shell.[13]

Teilhard would translate the political slogans of the French Revolution, liberty, equality, fraternity, into a new program for terrestrial man based on a new triad—universalism, futurism, personalism.[14]

Up to this point we have been concerned solely with the elucidation of a problematic—the problematic of a fragmented humanity emerging in a state of multiplicity aggravated by an innate tendency towards an individualistic egoism. We have also seen the inadequate response offered to this problematic by the various limited and also ambiguous forms of love which lie at the basis of man's communities. We have further seen that what is required in Teilhard's view is a universal form of love which will transcend the limitations of all the other forms at the same time that it cuts through their ambiguities, thus liberating them from their own perversions. The question remains: how can such a love be achieved and, even more fundamentally, is such a love even possible in the first place? However, before we can profitably explore Teilhard's own response to this question, we must first of all look at another aspect of the problem of the socialization or planetization of mankind. Having begun with the problem of love, we have at the same time begun with what Teilhard calls "the internal forces of unification." We must now see how these are related to the external forces of unification. This aspect of the problem of unity will allow us to see how Teilhard transposes the matter/spirit relationship into the context of socialization and, concomitantly, how he has developed in his later writings an aspect of the theory of creative union.

External and Internal Forces of Unification

Basic to the external forces bringing mankind into closer and closer proximity and hence at least raising the question of a necessary unification of the whole human race is the simple fact of what Teilhard calls "the roundness of the earth," the necessity for humankind to develop within the confines of a closed sphere.[15]

Teilhard usually rejected as very unlikely the possibility that interplanetary travel might eventually destroy the effectiveness of this factor as the basis of human compression.[16] However, he did at times allow for the outside chance that communication between different planetary noospheres might take place, thus prolonging the process of socialization beyond the frontiers of the earth into a process of cosmic socialization. However, Teilhard is always quick to add that the shape of the future would remain essentially the same, even if the perspective would be immeasurably broadened, and that as a result the end would only be postponed, not eliminated.[17] Teilhard is really forced into such a qualified admission by his conviction that the existence of life on other planets is quite probable.[18]

Beginning, then, with the earth as a closed sphere, Teilhard simply adds to this basic factor the population explosion and the technological complexification of the earth's surface to round out his treatment of the external forces of unification. Given the necessity of humanity's development over a limited area of space together with a rapidly expanding population and an increasingly complex network of lines of communication, humanity is driven quite inexorably towards greater and greater interdependence. Even against its own will, humanity is being forced into a kind of unity, even if such a unity is only external or tangential to begin with. The type of unity achieved by external forces is insufficient for the completion of the evolutionary movement, but it nonetheless plays an indispensable role in the development of that type of unity which can only be achieved by the internal forces of unification, notably love. Hence, similar to the role of matter in the genesis of spirit, the role of the external forces is to provide the matrix or fundamental conditions necessary for the flowering of that universal love in the spirit which alone is sufficient for the full unification of the noosphere. As we move deeper into this thematic from different points of view, we will have occasion to note that it is not so much a question of either external forces or internal forces but rather a question of their mutual interdependence. Both forces work together to unify mankind, but with the ascendency of the internal forces of unification (that is with the ascendency of the spirit) the external forces will gradually become less compulsive and more freely directed by the very forces of love at work in the noosphere. If the external forces of unification initially represent forces which are passively submitted to, they eventually become forces actively employed to foster the growth of the internal forces of unification.

We may conclude this section with one observation relevant to the theory of creative union. The theory of creative union seeks to express the relationship between matter and spirit in terms of passivity and activity, matter being that which is passively united, spirit that which actively unites. This process of the active unification of a passive multiplicity is properly creative in Teilhard's view inasmuch as God's creative activity appears to us under the form of an evolutionary process of unification. With the step of reflection, the appearance of man, the creative activity of God does not cease but rather assumes a new modality. Man is placed in the situation of being both that which is united and that which unites. Man is thus created both by the external and the internal forces of unification. Gradually, however, man becomes increasingly active in his own creation and hence less passive with respect to the external forces of unification which he is able now to control to a greater extent. The growth of unifying spirit (the internal forces) in the noosphere resembles the growth of spirit in the biosphere where spirit becomes increasingly discernible and active. This is, of course, exactly what we are led to expect from the typological methodology employed by Teilhard.

Teilhard conceived of mankind as both the matter and spirit of noospheric creation, as both that which is passively united and that which actively unites. In some sense, yet to be defined, the external and internal forces of unification translate for us the creative activity of God in the noosphere. We may leave this line of argument for the moment and proceed to see how Teilhard conceived of the spirit/matter relationship in its more usual sense in the context of noospheric development.

The Law of Complexity-Consciousness

The law of complexity-consciousness is a law of recurrence, and hence it holds good not only in the biosphere but in the noosphere

as well. The external forces of unification, particularly technological development, represent a process of complexification
necessitating a corresponding growth in consciousness. However,
in the noosphere, since complexification becomes collective or
planetary in nature, consciousness also develops as a collective or
planetary reality.

The genesis of higher forms of consciousness in the noosphere is
tied to the increasing complexification of the material matrix which
provides the conditioning base for the growth of spirit. However,
inasmuch as the complexification of the material focus is a work of
technological effort, that is a specifically human activity, man holds
in his own hands the power to heighten his level of collective awareness by further complexifying the network of interconnections
which increasingly draw the noosphere into unity. In other words,
at the stage of noogenesis in evolution, spirit becomes more and
more active in the process of its own genesis. This is what Teilhard
refers to as the "rebound effect," which is based on man's power of
invention.[19] To "reflective invention has fallen the role of prolonging, through planned and combined effort, the psychogenic process
of arrangement in which life consists."[20] From having been "at its
origins a *selective* process, evolution cannot but help become
gradually an *elective* process with the appearance of the higher
life-forms."[21] As an elective process, evolution can now be characterized as a process of auto- or self-evolution[22] because "man is
evolution become conscious of itself,"[23] and hence evolution is a
process now capable of being directed purposively from within.
Invention is precisely this power of purposive direction in man.

This power of invention in man lies at the basis of what Teilhard
terms the "rebound effect" in evolution. "In the first phase of
evolution, the more or less automatic genesis of man; then, in the
second phase of evolution, the rebound, the prolongation of evolution by means of artifacts collectively achieved by man...."[24]
Teilhard employs the image of a multistage rocket to clarify what
he means by the rebound effect:

I believe that what is now being shaped in the bosom of planetized
humanity is essentially a *rebounding* of evolution upon itself. We are
all familiar with projectiles whose impetus is renewed by the firing of a
series of staged rockets. Some such procedure, it seems to me, is what
life is preparing at this moment, to accomplish the supreme, ultimate

stage. The first stage was the elaboration of lower organisms, up to and including man, by the use and irrational combination of elementary sources of energy received or released by the planet. The second stage is the super-evolution of man, individually and collectively, by the use of refined forms of energy scientifically harnessed and applied in the bosom of the noosphere, thanks to the coordinated efforts of all men working reflectively and unanimously upon themselves. . . . This is life setting out upon a second adventure from the springboard it established when it created mankind.[25]

The stage of human rebound in evolution introduces an important modification into the relationship between complexity and consciousness: "So we may say that . . . by a sort of chain-reaction, consciousness, itself born of complexity, finds itself in a position to bring about 'artificially' a further increase of complexity in its material dwelling (thus engendering and liberating a further growth of reflective consciousness, and so on . . .)."[26] In line with this argument, it is proper to say that "an auto-cerebration of humanity becomes the most succinct expression of the reflective rebound of evolution"[27] inasmuch as the network of technologically achieved interconnections within humanity constitute in some sense an immense collective brain.[28] This analogy is quite in keeping with the theme of cerebration or cephalization as a parameter of developing consciousness in the earlier stages of evolution.[29]

It is with the interrelated themes of invention and rebound that we see most clearly the development of the dialectic of activity and passivity used by Teilhard in his theory of creative union to delineate the relationship between spirit and matter. Whatever unifying role spirit may play at the pre-human stages of evolution (and Teilhard does argue in favor of the presence of certain inventive capacities in the pre-human stages of evolution[30]), the unifying role of spirit becomes most evident with man in the area of his socializing activity. The *emphasis* in evolution has now shifted to the focus of consciousness and away from the focus of complexification in the genesis of spirit. We are now in a position to see how some of these themes affect Teilhard's understanding of the relationship between tangential and radial energy in the context of socialization.

Tangential and Radial Energy

As we remarked when treating this theme in Chapter II, the notion of tangential and radial energy becomes terminologically precise only with the writing of *The Phenomenon of Man*. Thus we begin again with this work for our present purposes.

By their very nature, and at every level of complexity, the elements of the world are able to influence and mutually penetrate each other through their within, so as to combine their "radial energy" in bundles. While no more than merely conjectural in atoms and molecules, this psychic interpenetrability grows and becomes directly perceptible in the case of organized beings. Finally, with the appearance of man in whom the effects of consciousness attain to their present maximal level in the world of nature, this psychic interpenetrability is everywhere present in an extreme degree and can be seen with particular clarity in all aspects of the phenomenon of socialization. Furthermore, we are capable of directly experiencing it for ourselves. But at the same time, in the case of man as in all other cases, this psychic interpenetrability depends for its effective operation upon certain "tangential energies" of arrangement and hence upon certain prior conditions of spatial rapprochement.[31]

The effective operation of the internal forces of unification, notably love, depends upon the prior and concomitant presence of the external forces of compression, notably the roundness of the earth, population explosion, and technological development, which serve to bring mankind into some kind of proximity. The external or tangential forces of collective complexification lead to a growth in consciousness or radial energy: "Mega-synthesis in the tangential, and therefore, *ipso facto*, a leap forward of the radial energies, following the principal axis of evolution. Increasing complexity and consequently growth in consciousness."[32]

In the years following the completion of *The Phenomenon of Man*, Teilhard uses this theme not so much to indicate the interdependence of tangential and radial energy in the development of the noosphere as to point up the inadequacy and even danger of the external forces of compression: "In virtue of the laws of molecularization, the problem obviously consists in finding the means of grouping ourselves together, not 'tangentially,' that is by means of activities or functions which bind us together only extrinsically, but rather 'radially,' that is *center to center*..."[33] Tangential relationships, precisely because they move on the periphery of man's interior life, tend to be depersonalizing and hence threatening. However essential tangential or external factors are as a basis for unification, they are fundamentally ambiguous. Unless the complexification of the material base of human socialization is inspired and directed by love and thus placed at the service of personalization, it becomes in the end merely destructive.

We have already seen that at the human phase of evolution consciousness becomes increasingly capable of complexifying its own material matrix and in this way contributing to its own further growth. An emphasis on the ambiguity of the tangential forces of unification makes it clear by implication that consciousness must be saved by love from a fundamental ambiguity present in its own seemingly constructive efforts in the world of matter. In other words, the law of complexity-consciousness as applied to the noosphere is not merely a law of development but also a law of ambiguous development. Not only is complexification ambiguous but consciousness, the artisan of complexification, is itself ambiguous. Both need to be directed away from their evil potentialities by love. And again we see that spirit and matter in the context of hominization are not simply to be opposed as directional vectors towards unity and multiplicity. Rather, both spirit and matter are ambiguous factors in the development of evolution. If matter is to be redeemed by spirit from its inherent tendency to multiplicity, spirit itself must first be redeemed from its own inherent ambiguities through a universal form of love, which must be activated by a force outside of and yet immanent in the socializing process itself. We hope to establish this point in the next chapter. However, we should first of all like to establish in more detail the correctness of our assertion that the development of the noosphere is an ambiguous development by investigating Teilhard's thinking on the notion of progress.

Progress

The law of complexity-consciousness provides us with a yardstick of progress—the progress in the complexification of matter being matched by a corresponding progress in consciousness. If we accept the basic premise that consciousness is better than unconscious-ness,[34] then we can say that the fundamental progress made in the universe is the growth of consciousness.

Can the law of complexity-consciousness as a gauge of progress also be used to determine if man is progressing? Undoubtedly our answer to this question must be affirmative.[35] However, even if it is true that consciousness has been growing throughout the history of life on this planet and that it has grown enormously from the initial appearance of man up to the present, will it continue to grow in the future? There are good reasons leading us to think so, according to Teilhard, but "if progress is to continue, it will not do so of its own accord. *Evolution, by the very mechanism of its synthesis, charges itself with an ever-growing measure of freedom.*"[36] With the appear-ance of man and particularly with the advent of the increased socialization of mankind, evolution becomes more and more a process of auto-evolution dependent upon man's commitment to its progressive continuation. The law of complexity-consciousness ceases, with the appearance of man, to function as an indicator of automatic advance and becomes rather a guide to the possible direction of the future, an option to be decided upon by man. Man now has it in his power to continue the work of complexification and thus promote the growth of consciousness in the noosphere, but he need not do so. Man's freedom must be activated by a vision of the future, a goal ahead, if it is to become committed to the laborious task of carrying the thrust of the evolutionary movement forward to completion. How this can be done will constitute the subject matter of the next chapter. However, for our present pur-poses, we should like simply to underline the fundamental ambiguity of the progress in consciousness convincingly demon-strated by Teilhard's argument in order to reinforce Teilhard's in-sistence on the capital role to be played by freedom in the continuation of evolution.

The technological advances made in the area of complexification and the concomitant growth of consciousness in man have in-credibly broadened the possibilities open to man in the present and in the future. Nonetheless, this growth in complexity-consciousness represents at the same time a growth in the possibilities for evil as well as for good, for greater destruction as well as for greater unity. In 1916, Teilhard writes:

We would like to be able... to hope that suffering and wickedness are only transitory conditions of the life-process, that science and the rise of civilization will eliminate them both some day. Let us be honest with ourselves and have the courage to look at the human condition as it really is. With the increasing development and complexification of humanity, opportunities for disorder simply multiply and at the same time their seriousness is severely aggravated. No one moves a mountain without simultaneously leaving a deep abyss and every form of energy is equally powerful for good and for evil. Everything which *becomes* suffers or sins. The truth about our situation in this world is that *we are nailed to a cross*.[37]

While Teilhard does not particularly emphasize the possibilities for evil present in the growth and progress of consciousness, he does recognize their existence.[38] More than this, his constant concern to emphasize the good possibilities in this progress and to encourage mankind to exploit these possibilities freely is motivated in part at least by a desire to see that mankind does not choose to exploit the evil possibilities ready to hand as a result of a failure to grasp what can lie ahead in the future for the human race. Teilhard is a visionary, if you will, but he is championing a vision of the future which he is convinced has a solid *fundamentum in re*. Teilhard's vision of the future arises out of an imaginative grasp of the real possibilities inherent in the present situation of the world, and he is concerned to motivate men to commit themselves to the actuation of these possibilities. If he does not endlessly rehearse all the evil possibilities whose actuation would cause his vision to fall to the ground, he should not be faulted for this, for his basic intent is to offer a viable option for the future. He has quite naturally marshaled all the evidence he can discover to show that his vision is not necessarily illusory and hence is capable of realization if pursued in earnest.

Something like a law of self-fulfilling prophecies perhaps illumines what Teilhard is saying. If mankind becomes convinced that the future is empty and settles back into an attitude of pessimism and despair, the future will indeed become empty because the shape of the future depends upon mankind's labor in constructing it. If, on the other hand, mankind becomes convinced that the future holds out the promise of further enrichment and if mankind becomes committed to the realization of these promises, then the future will indeed be full because the shape of the future lies in large measure in man's own hands.

If Teilhard frequently seems much more assured of the direction of the future than this line of argument would suggest, it is for reasons which are not basically scientific but rather theological. But even the theological arguments which he advances to guarantee the success of evolution do not undermine this fundamental insistence on the role to be played by human freedom and responsibility in the ultimate success of evolution. Teilhard *does* take freedom seriously and he *does* take its ambiguity seriously, but he also takes with utmost seriousness theological factors activating freedom as we shall see in the next chapter. But before pushing on into the theological area of Teilhard's argument, we may summarize the results of the present chapter.

Summary

We have been concerned with the problem of the one and the many as a human problem, as a problem of the socialization of mankind. We have seen that the appearance of man in the world inaugurates a new movement of multiplicity in evolution and hence that mankind constitutes a new multiplicity to be unified. We have tried to indicate the role played in this process of unification both by external forces of compression, such as the roundness of the earth, the population explosion, and technological development, and by internal forces of unification, particularly love. In sum, this chapter can best be described as the analysis of a problematic, a problematic created by the ambiguity of the forces of unification, whether external or internal. External forces of unification are basically ambiguous because, while they do in fact bring mankind into at least a geographical unity, they also tend to be depersonalizing. The external forces of compression constitute the *sine qua non* material matrix for a deeper kind of unity, but in and of themselves they are ambiguous, and when divorced from the internal forces of unification they are positively dangerous because they threaten the person. The profoundest kind of unity among men can only be achieved by love, that is, by a relationship between centers; but love, in all its limited forms, is itself a fundamentally ambiguous unitive force because in the process of uniting it also tends to divide. All the forms of love observable in the noosphere—whether in the form of sexual attraction, friendship, patriotism, or whatever —are limited in character and hence tend to create islands of unity which finally constitute simply more grandiose forms of fragmentation.

What is needed is a universal love, a love transcending all the limited forms of love in the noosphere even if at the same time it takes its point of departure from the positive values inherent in these limited forms. Such a universal love would not only purify all the limited forms of love from their ambiguity and draw all men into internal unity but it would at the same time purify the external forces of unification, particularly technology, from their ambiguity by placing them at the service of the growth of persons in unity.

Such is the problematic and such is the proposed answer to this problematic. The question is where are we to discover the means of achieving that universal form of love which alone can redeem us from our impasse? We must now search with Teilhard for the answer to this final, all important question.

Christ: Omega

We saw in the previous chapter that in Teilhard's mind only a universal form of love is capable of both simultaneously unifying and personalizing the multiplicity of mankind in a truly organic unity. We concluded our last chapter with a question: how is such a universal love to be activated in mankind? However, before we can explore the rather complex way in which Teilhard seeks to answer this question, we must first note a fundamental objection to his position in this regard, an objection to which Teilhard was quite sensitive, as the following text from *The Phenomenon of Man* indicates:

Mankind, the spirit of the earth, the synthesis of individuals and peoples, the paradoxical reconciliation of the part with the whole and of unity with multiplicity—all these are spoken of as being nothing more than utopian dreams and yet at the same time their realization is recognized as being biologically necessary. For these "dreams" to become concrete realities in the world all we may well have to do is to imagine our power of loving developing until it embraces the totality of mankind as well as the totality of the cosmos.

Now it may be objected at this point that it is precisely on this score that my whole scheme falls to the ground.

A man can only give his love to a small circle of intimates. A man's heart is simply not large enough to carry him beyond the radius of that small circle, outside of which there is room for only the cold objectivity of reason and justice. To love the whole cosmos and every other human

being in it is a meaningless and ridiculous enterprise, which leads in
the end to loving nothing.[1]

But Teilhard refuses to back down in the face of these objections
which call into question the very possibility of achieving the love
he deems biologically essential:

We are often inclined to think that we have exhausted the various
natural forms of love with a man's love for his wife, his children, his
friends, and to a certain extent for his country. Yet precisely the most
fundamental form of passion is missing from this list, the one which,
under the pressure of a coiling universe, precipitates the elements one
upon the other in the whole—cosmic affinity and hence the cosmic
sense.

A universal love is not only psychologically possible; it is the only
complete and final way in which we are able to love.[2]

How, then, is such a universal love to be achieved?

In order for the failure that now threatens us to be transformed into
victory, for the conspiration of the human monads to be realized, it is
necessary and sufficient for us that we extend our scientific efforts to
their farthest limits and accept as well as recognize (as being necessary
to the stabilization and finalization of the space-time continuum) not
only some vague future existence, but also, and on this point I must
insist with all possible emphasis, the reality and now present activity
of that mysterious Center of all centers to whom I have given the name
Omega.[3]

The Omega Point

The difficulty in attempting to understand what Teilhard means by
the term "Omega" derives from the simple fact that he does not
mean one thing alone by it.[4] In what follows we should like to argue
that in fact Teilhard assigns four distinct but intimately interrelated
senses to the term "Omega."

In the first place, the "Omega Point" designates the final unity of
mankind on itself, a state of coreflection which will bring to completion the movement of unification by external and internal forces
already observable in the noosphere. This final unity of all mankind
we may call the first sense of "Omega," and it functions as a virtual
center of convergence in that it exists only as a future ideal which
does not as yet exist even if it is in process of realization. This first
sense of "Omega" constitutes what Teilhard refers to as the

"collectivist solution"[5] or the "solution of the Marxist type"[6] to the problem of socialization. It might also be called the "secularist solution" in that it is basically atheistic in its presuppositions. While this initial solution to the problem of mankind's unity does serve to some extent to activate that universal form of love necessary for the success of evolution, it is ultimately seen to be insufficiently activating and hence incomplete as a final solution to the basic problem of unification. An analysis of Teilhard's reasons for rejecting as insufficient this first sense of "Omega" will lead us to the second sense in which he understands the term.

The fatal flaw in the collectivist solution to socialization, in Teilhard's mind, is its inability to deal adequately with the problem of mankind's death at the end. The collectivist solution cannot guarantee the irreversibility (which for Teilhard means the immortality) of the evolutionary movement of man, and hence it cannot ultimately sustain man's desire to carry the evolutionary movement forward to completion. If only death awaits all our efforts, then an irreducible absurdity is introduced into human activity. As Teilhard writes to Henri Breuil in March of 1934 shortly after the death of his friend and colleague Davidson Black:

But what an absurd thing life is, looked at superficially: so absurd that you feel yourself forced back on a stubborn, desperate faith in the reality and survival of the spirit. Otherwise—were there no such thing as spirit, I mean—we should be idiots not to call off the whole of human effort.[7]

Only the conviction that evolution is an irreversible movement which finally saves persons from the annihilation of death can serve as a viable basis for the action required to keep man moving into the future towards unity.[8] And in order to guarantee the irreversibility of the thrust towards human unity, it is necessary to postulate the existence of a personal Center up ahead who can function as the collector of persons beyond the death barrier.

The two senses of "Omega" thus far elaborated do not stand in contradiction to one another. Rather, the second sense of "Omega," as the transcendent personal Center of evolution, completes the logic of Teilhard's understanding of Omega as the unity of mankind on itself by correcting its personalistic inadequacies and reinforcing its activating potentialities in relation to human activity.

4

Geometrically speaking, the first sense of "Omega" may be represented by the figure of a circle symbolizing the unity of mankind on itself, a unity arrived at by an immanentist movement of mankind which rejects any possibility of intervention from outside; while the second sense of "Omega" may be represented by the same circle complemented and completed by the introduction of a center point, a point which is transcendent in that it is not the product of evolution itself but rather its ground and guarantee.

Whereas the first sense of "Omega" constitutes an ideal and hence virtual center of largely psychological attraction, "Omega" understood in the second sense constitutes a real and hence actual center of both psychological and ontological attraction in that the transcendent, personal Omega Point is able to act within the history of being not only motivating it towards unity but, what is more important, actually bringing it to unity by his personal influence. Teilhard's transcendent, personal Center resembles the unknown God of the Athenians, whom St. Paul identified for his Greek listeners as none other than Jesus Christ (Acts 17, 22–34). This Center is the God of evolution, whose attributes may be arrived at by reason from an analysis of the exigencies of the evolutionary movement[9] (cf. Romans 1, 18–23), but who is as yet unnamed. The very fact that Teilhard has recourse to the use of the Greek letter "Omega" indicates that he wishes to begin with what is initially but a symbol of ultimacy and finality, the content of which he will gradually clarify in ascending steps.

The Christ-Omega

Teilhard has thus far been working in the area of religious apologetics, attempting to establish both the necessity of the immortality of the soul as a prerequisite for action and the existence of God as a prerequisite for immortality. The arguments establishing a transcendent, personal God as the center of unity of mankind constitute in essence an apologetic effort to establish the existence of God in a new evolutionary framework of thought.[10] But Teilhard, like Paul (in so many ways Teilhard's teacher), does not rest content with the logical postulate of an unknown God of evolution. For in the third stage of his dialectic he goes on to identify this Center with Jesus Christ, who thus represents the third sense of "Omega."

In 1953, Teilhard speaks of a certain correspondence between these two understandings of "Omega":

Is not the correspondence between the figure (the "pattern") of the two Omegas at hand rather revealing? The one postulated by modern science, the other experienced by Christian mysticism? The correspondence, or even the identity! [11]

What Teilhard hopes is that if humanity can become convinced of the necessity of a transcendent pole of unification and also become accustomed to thinking of Jesus Christ in terms of his cosmic attributes and functions, eventually a synthesis between the two Omegas will take place.[12] It was in order to bring this eventual synthesis about that Teilhard labored for so many years to develop christological dogma in the direction of a truly cosmic understanding of Christ's attributes and functions by emphasizing certain aspects of Johannine and particularly Pauline christology.[13]

What Teilhard needed from christology was a Christ who could be correlated (or as Teilhard would say, made to cohere) with the transcendent personal pole of evolution which could be arrived at on the basis of an inspection of the requirements for the final unity of mankind. In other words, Teilhard developed christological dogma in a quite particular direction for apologetic reasons, to make the Christ of Christian faith relevant to the evolutionary mentality and needs of the modern world. Teilhard was convinced that if he could once persuade the unbeliever to accept the necessity of a transcendent, personal God as the completion of the logic of "Omega" understood as the final unity of mankind, he could then go on to show the correlation between the second sense of "Omega" and a third sense of "Omega" (Jesus Christ), provided that an appropriate understanding of Jesus Christ already existed in advance to be correlated with the second sense of "Omega."

While Teilhard does not go to great lengths to demonstrate that his own personal cosmic christology is in fact traditional in its roots, he does keep insisting that he has only developed in the context of an evolutionary world view a line of christological reflection which already exists in John, Paul, and the Greek Fathers. Now his insistence on this point is of crucial importance *for apologetical reasons* inasmuch as the unbeliever could always contend that, however attractive Teilhard's christological proposals might be,

Universitas
BIBLIOTHECA
Ottaviensis

they represented, in the last analysis, but a private interpretation of Christianity and hence had no validity as an argument in favor of the viability of Christianity as the religion of the future.

Surely, one of the reasons why Teilhard was so anxious to have his christological views accepted within the Church was that such an acceptance would give him, and, what is more important, would give the Church a stronger base from which to carry on this effort of correlation on behalf of the unbeliever. Teilhard felt it was imperative that the Church at large begin to develop a christological line of reflection which was both traditional, if somewhat neglected, and at the same time relevant to the contemporary world. Teilhard wished only to be a spokesman to the world for authentic Christianity, but he was totally unable to acquiesce in what he personally (and for good objective reasons) was convinced was a rather narrow, reactionary interpretation of what authentic Christianity actually consisted in. While not denying the validity of other christological emphases, Teilhard focused on the cosmic aspects of christology for apologetic and personal reasons. In short, Teilhard was not concerned to work out a complete systematic theology (for which task he was hardly suited in the first place), but rather to highlight certain aspects of theology which could be correlated with a contemporary evolutionary world view.

The Church-Omega

If we may retrace our steps for a moment, we have seen thus far that Teilhard understands the "Omega Point" in three senses: first of all, "Omega" represents the unity of mankind on itself (the secularist interpretation); secondly, "Omega" represents a transcendent personal Center of unity towards whom mankind converges and in whom it finds immortality and fulfillment in unity (the theistic interpretation); in the third place, "Omega" represents Jesus Christ, considered from the perspective of his cosmic attributes and functions as the transcendent personal Center of unity (the christological interpretation). The emphasis in the first sense of "Omega" falls on the human race as a collective unity, whereas the emphasis in the second and third senses of "Omega" falls on the personal Center of this collective unity. Thus in order to balance the correlation between the various senses of "Omega," we may add a fourth sense which represents the mystical Body of Christ in its fulfillment at the end-time (the ecclesiological interpretation). The emphasis in this fourth sense once again falls upon the collectivity of mankind, but from the point of view of the members of the human race as members of the Body of Christ. The fourth sense of "Omega" then correlates with the first in much the same way as the third sense correlates with the second.

We have already seen that in order to establish a correlation between the theistic and christological interpretations of "Omega," Teilhard was forced to develop christological dogma in the direction of the cosmic attributes and functions of Christ which he was convinced (and with reason) had already been adumbrated in biblical and patristic christologies. The question may now be asked whether Teilhard was also compelled to develop ecclesiological dogma in the same direction? What this would mean concretely is that Teilhard would have to shift the emphasis in ecclesiology away from the hierarchical and sacramental structures of the Church (which have traditionally been predominant in ecclesiological treatises particularly since the time of the Reformation) in the direction of the Church's role in furthering the progress of cosmic evolution. We might just note before attempting to answer this question that it is not necessary for Teilhard to deny traditional emphases in ecclesiology in order to develop a cosmic ecclesiology, any more than it was necessary for him to deny traditional emphases in christology in order to develop a cosmic christology. What one would expect to happen, judging from the analogy with christology, is that Teilhard would leave traditional emphases largely in the shade because they cohere with a complex of questions which have ceased to be urgent and meaningful for an increasingly large segment of contemporary humanity. The Reformation problematic vis-à-vis ecclesiology continues to be relevant in the context of current ecumenical discussions among the churches, but as soon as ecumenism is broadened to include dialogue with the world, which is precisely the way in which Teilhard understood ecumenism,[14] then the ecclesiological problematic is changed and the notion of the Church has to be dealt with in a different way. In order to see how Teilhard develops ecclesiology, we must first see how Teilhard understands the activating power of Omega (in all its various senses) in relation to that universal form of love which we have seen is necessary for the final success of evolution.

The Activating Power of Omega

One of the clearest instances of the method of correlation of the various senses of "Omega" in relation to the problem of activating a universal love can be seen in the very structure as well as the argumentation of *The Phenomenon of Man*. The bulk of the study is devoted to the analysis of the phenomenon of man as the title indicates. However, Teilhard appended to this an epilogue on the Christian phenomenon precisely in order to correlate the two phenomena. Let us see, then, how Teilhard carries out his program of correlation in *The Phenomenon of Man*.

In a section entitled "The Attributes of Point Omega" Teilhard has this to say of the role of Omega in relation to the problem of love:

Expressed in terms of internal energy, the cosmic function of Omega consists in initiating and maintaining within its radius the unanimity of the world's "reflective" particles. But how could it exercise this action were it not in some way loving and lovable *at this very moment*? Love, I have said, dies in contact with the impersonal and the anonymous. With equal infallibility it becomes impoverished with remoteness in space—and still more, much more, with remoteness in time. For love to be possible there must be coexistence. Accordingly, however marvelous its foreseen figure, Omega could never even so much as equilibrate the play of human attractions and repulsions if it did not act with equal force, that is to say with the same sort of proximity. With love, as with every other type of energy, it is within the existing situation that the lines of force must at every instant come together. Neither an ideal center, nor a potential center could possibly suffice. A present and real noosphere requires a real and present center. To be supremely attractive, Omega must be supremely present.[15]

"Love, I have said, dies in contact with the impersonal and the anonymous . . . Neither an ideal center, nor a potential center could possibly suffice." With these lines Teilhard eliminates the unity of mankind on itself as a definitive interpretation of the "Omega Point" because it is shown to be insufficiently activating in terms of love. For reasons of love, then, it is necessary that Omega be present, not just potential. Omega must be both loving and lovable, and undoubtedly in a supereminent way, in order to overcome the forces of repulsion (individualism?) at work in the noosphere. With this line of argument Teilhard hopes to establish the necessity of the existence of a transcendent, personal God for the success of the movement of human unification through love.

We may now turn to the Epilogue to see how Teilhard handles the correlation between the second and third senses of "Omega."

It is already quite plain in Paul and John that to create, to fulfill, and to purify the world is equivalent, for God, to unifying it by uniting it organically to himself. How does he unify it? By partially immersing himself in things, by becoming an "element" in the whole, and then, from this vantage point at the heart of matter, assuming the leadership and control of what we now call evolution. Christ, the universal principle of vitalization because he was born into the world as a man among men, placed himself in a position (maintained ever since) to subdue, to purify, to direct, and to superanimate the general ascent of consciousnesses into which he had inserted himself. By a perennial act of communion and sublimation, he aggregates to himself the total psychism of the earth. And when he has gathered everything together and transformed everything, he will close in upon himself and his conquests, thereby rejoining, in a final gesture, the divine focus he has never really left. Then as St. Paul tells us, *God shall be all in all*. This is indeed a superior form of "pantheism" without trace of the poison of adulteration or annihilation: the expectation of perfect unity, immersed in which each element will reach its consummation at the same time as the universe does.

The universe fulfilling itself in a synthesis of centers in perfect conformity with the laws of union. God, the Center of centers. In that final vision Christian dogma finds its culmination. And so exactly, so perfectly does this coincide with the Omega Point that doubtless I should never have ventured to envisage the latter or formulate the hypothesis rationally if, in my consciousness as a believer, I had not found not only its speculative model but also its living reality.[16]

Before Teilhard can hope to correlate Christ with the transcendent, personal Center arrived at as a rational hypothesis, he has to set out a particular understanding of Christ which, while not ignoring by any means his historical existence among men, concentrates on his functions as Pantocrator and Consummator, a thematic reminiscent of Greek patristic christology and explicitly related by

Teilhard to the christologies of Paul and John. Having provided himself with an appropriate christological platform, Teilhard then goes on to proclaim the striking coincidence between the Christ believed in and worshiped within the Christian phenomenon and the Omega arrived at earlier in his analysis of the exigencies of evolution. This he does by making the admission that the model of the cosmic Christ undoubtedly conditioned his presentation of the attributes of his transcendent, personal Center, although at the same time he insists by implication on the validity of his rational arguments establishing the existence of such a Center quite apart from Christian revelation.

In other words, Teilhard admits that the shape of his answer conditioned to some extent the structure of his question. However, it should be kept in mind that in the actual development of Teilhard's own thought, the question and answer mutually influenced one another inasmuch as his research into evolution served to broaden his christological perspectives at the same time that his widening christological reflections served to deepen his understanding of the nature and meaning of evolution. Nonetheless, Teilhard's admission at this point is of capital importance in understanding the motive of his method of correlation in that it underlines with unmistakable clarity the priority of its theological ground. We shall return to this point a little later.

The Probability of a Revelation from Omega

In order to tighten the logic of Teilhard's argument before passing on to consider his development of ecclesiology, we may just note that his jump from the phenomenon of man to the Christian phenomenon is not quite as arbitrary as it may seem at first sight. For, as an integral part of his effort to link together the theistic and christological interpretations of "Omega," he regularly tries to establish the antecedent probability of a revelation from the transcendent, personal Center he has established by rational argument. This is of course standard apologetical procedure, but, given the new context in which the whole of Teilhard's apologetical theology operates, his argumentation takes on a certain freshness and force. In the Epilogue to *The Phenomenon of Man*, for example, which

we are presently considering, Teilhard makes this allusion to the
probability of a revelation:

If, on the other hand, Omega is, as we have admitted, *already in
existence* and operative at the very core of the thinking mass, then it
would seem inevitable that traces of its existence should be manifested
to us here and now. To animate evolution at its lower stages, the
conscious pole of the world could of course only act in an impersonal
form and under the veil of biology. Upon the thinking entity that we
have become by hominization, it is now possible for it to radiate from
the one center to all centers—*personally*. Would it seem likely that it
should not do so?[17]

Once the existence of Omega as the transcendent personal Center
of the converging movement of evolution has been postulated, then
the possibility of his revealing his presence becomes antecedently
probable and it also becomes reasonable for man to begin searching
for traces of this revelation in his own history.

Such a search would inevitably lead the concerned questioner to
a study of the history of religions and particularly to a comparative
analysis of their respective attitudes to the evolutionary movement
of the world understood principally as a movement of amorization
and personalization culminating in the unity of finite personal
centers in a transcendent personal Center.

Let us just briefly see how Teilhard applies this method in one
of his most important apologetical essays, "Comment je crois,"
written in 1934 at the request of his friend Bruno de Solages. Teilhard begins by saying that "in traditional apologetics, the choice
of a religion was principally determined by the consideration of
miracles."[18] He goes on to say that he has no particular difficulty
personally with the notion of miracles, but that he does not find
the argument based upon such a consideration especially cogent
and hence would prefer to work out his own apologetic from a
different perspective.

The only reason capable of leading me to give my adherence to a
religion would be the superior harmony existing between this religion
and the personal creed to which I have been led by the natural evolution of my faith.[19]

Faith in the unity of the world, faith in the existence and the immortality of the spirit born from the synthesis of the world. These three
articles of my creed are in turn all summed up for me in the adoration
of a personal and personalizing center of universal convergence.[20]

On the basis of this personal creed Teilhard feels that he is in a position to undertake a comparative analysis of religions. This turns out to be quite rudimentary and we need not follow Teilhard in his rejection of first the Oriental religions and secondly what he calls the "various forms of humanitarian pantheism" (for example, Marxism).[21] His remarks with respect to Christianity are, on the other hand, of some interest.

He begins with this rather surprising observation:

I have, therefore, given myself up to the influence of the Church. Not, however, as the result of some cleverly contrived mental gymnastics, but rather after a prolonged attempt to make my own insignificant personal religion coincide with the great religion of Jesus. To be perfectly honest with myself, I must admit that I was forced to conclude a third time, as with the other religious options, that no genuine accord in fact existed between the two—at least at the beginning. I did not at first recognize myself in the mirror of the gospel.[22]

The basic reason for this, Teilhard tells us, was that "Christianity did not seem to believe in human progress. It had not developed, or perhaps had simply allowed to lie dormant within itself, the sense of the earth."[23] Teilhard's own personal difficulties with the Christianity (that is Catholicism) with which he was familiar clearly resume a whole line of nineteenth-century objections to Christianity which found most notable expression in the critiques of Marx and Nietzsche. In order for Teilhard to become an intellectually committed Christian it was necessary for him to see a side of the Christian tradition which was relegated to the shadowy background of the life of the Church at the beginning of the present century. But once he saw it he knew that it was what he had been looking for and, furthermore, he knew that it was this side of Christianity which had now to be developed and made to stand in the foreground of the Church's life if the Church were ever going to be relevant to the twentieth century. Since the answer which he had found satisfied the exigencies of his own personal problematic, which seemed to coincide in large measure with the problematic of a large sector of the educated contemporary world, would it not be logical to assume that this answer would also be relevant to that world?

What exactly was the answer which Teilhard found to his difficulties?

Were the exigencies of my own personal religion so exceptional and so new that no traditional formula could satisfy them?

Such indeed seemed to be the case.

And then the universal Christ suddenly made his appearance.

The universal Christ, such as I personally understand him at any rate, is a synthesis of Christ and the universe. Not a new divinity, but rather the inevitable interpretation of that mystery in which the whole of Christianity is crystallized: the incarnation.[24]

The God of Christianity, Jesus Christ, is not a local god, the god of a private esoteric cult, but rather the God of evolution, the God of the entire cosmos, and it is this God whom Christianity believes in and worships. Such is the faith of Teilhard and the reason for his adherence to Catholic Christianity. With the reintroduction of the cosmic or universal Christ we are brought full circle back to our consideration of the various senses of "Omega." and we may now resume the thread of our argument from the Epilogue of *The Phenomenon of Man*.

The Cosmic Function of the Church

We may now ask how Teilhard understands the role of the Church in the perspective of evolutionary history:

It is a phenomenon of capital importance for the science of man that, over an appreciable region of the earth, a zone of thought has appeared and grown in which a genuinely universal love has not only been conceived and preached, but has also been shown to be psychologically possible and operative in practice. It is all the more capital inasmuch as, far from decreasing, the movement seems to desire only to gain still greater momentum and intensity.[25]

It is considerably more important to see that the Church is the locus of love in the world than to see that it is a highly organized system of rites and beliefs:

Is it not a fact, as I can warrant, that if the love of God were extinguished in the souls of the faithful, the enormous edifice of rites, of hierarchy and of doctrines that comprise the Church would instantly revert to the dust from which it arose?[26]

This is not to suggest that the hierarchical, sacramental, and doctrinal structures of the Church are unimportant or unnecessary, but rather that they depend upon love for their vitality and effectiveness, and that they exist as a service to the growth of that universal love which is of the essence of the gospel and of the life of the Christian community. Teilhard is concerned to accent that facet of the Church's life which is most pertinent to his own understanding of the present and future needs of evolutionary history, but it could hardly be said that he has fixed on what is merely an incidental or peripheral aspect of that life in the interests of his apologetical purposes.

For Teilhard the Church is principally a "phylum of love,"[27] and as the locus of universal love it constitutes the axis of the evolutionary movement as it drives towards its future fulfillment. The value Teilhard sees in this approach to the Church is that the very existence of the Church as a phylum of love proves that a universal love, such as he had already shown to be necessary, is not only psychologically possible, but, what is more important, is now historically and hence concretely operative within the noosphere. This argument is designed to silence those skeptics who claim that a universal love is unrealizable.

The Church as a phylum of love fills a void, it assumes its proper place in the history of evolution, it is exactly what evolutionists have been looking for.

I have tried to show that we can hope for no progress on earth apart from the primacy and the triumph of the *personal* at the summit of *spirit*. And at the present moment Christianity is the *unique* current of thought within the entire noosphere which is sufficiently audacious and sufficiently progressive to lay hold of the world at the level of effective practice in an embrace at once already complete, and yet capable of indefinite perfection, where faith and hope attain their fulfillment in love. *Alone*, unconditionally alone in the world today, Christianity shows itself able to reconcile in a single living act the All and the person. Alone, it can bend our hearts not only to the service of that tremendous movement of the world which bears us along, but even beyond it to embrace that movement in love.

In other words, can we not say that Christianity fulfills all the conditions we are entitled to expect from a religion of the future; and that hence, through it, the principal axis of evolution truly passes, as it maintains?[28]

Teilhard's own experiences in the Church could hardly have served to create any illusions in his mind about the actual state of the Church. That the Church did not present itself effectively and credibly to the world as a community of love at the service of the world's ongoing progress was well enough known to Teilhard. In fact, he was only too painfully aware of the fact. A text like the one just cited is not only an apologetic outburst which may well seem to idealize unduly the actual face of the Church, but it is at the same time a challenge to the Church itself to develop in a more credible fashion what it is in fact meant to be. Teilhard was aware that his own understanding of christology and ecclesiology was not exactly at the forefront of the Church's present thought and life, but he also realized that his own understanding of these areas was deeply rooted in the Christian tradition. He was urging the Church to develop precisely those aspects of christology and ecclesiology which were integral to its tradition in order that it might manifest itself to the world as the looked-for axis which he was convinced it in fact is.

Just as Teilhard had the Christ model in mind as he worked out the attributes and functions of Omega in a rational form from an inspection of the exigencies of the future of evolution, so too he had the Christian model of love in mind as he worked out the attributes and function of universal love in a rational form from an inspection of the exigencies of noogenesis. This he freely admits himself.[29] The correlation between a universal form of love and Christian charity enables him to give a name to his postulate, just as his correlation between Christ and Omega understood as a transcendent personal Center enables him to name the latter. The method of correlation, therefore, provides a passageway from the anonymity of a postulate to the concreteness of an actually existing and known reality. The help which Teilhard derives from his own faith-experience does not *ipso facto* invalidate the legitimacy of his rational analysis of the movement of evolution and its future exigencies in that his evolutionary system, even as extrapolated into the future, possess a coherence and cogency quite apart from his subsequent efforts to correlate it with Christian faith. And for Teilhard, such coherence constitutes the test of truth.[30]

Again we should note that, if it is true that the answers influence the way in which the questions are asked, the questions also influence the shape of the answers given. Teilhard does not really begin with ready-made answers derived from faith or theology. He himself admits, as we have seen, that the theology with which he was familiar at the beginning of the century did not at first seem to cohere at all with his own religious problematic. The pressure of his needs drove him to develop his theological understanding in a direction appropriate to the questions which were urgent to him. This point emerges clearly from his description of Christian charity. His model of universal love was not derived from the notion of Christian charity as he felt it had traditionally been understood. In fact, he is frequently critical of the understanding of Christian charity to which he had been exposed and which he believed to be rather limited in scope. The following text from 1929 is typical:

The charity spoken of in the gospel has too long remained that of the good Samaritan, who welcomes, heals, and consoles. Is there really no room to give this magnificent virtue a form which would be still more generous and active? Alongside the soldier who is solicitous for his wounded comrade, there is also to be found the soldier whose devotion consists in carrying forward the assault without let-up. Love of neighbor could not, of course, let fall this flower of compassion which has given rise to such an impressive harvest of charitable enterprises without at the same time losing something of its intrinsic beauty. Nonetheless, love of neighbor has now to assume a more solid form through a passionate attachment to the overall work of the world. Not only to bring relief, but to develop. Not only to make reparation, but to build. Love of neighbor at this point in history can signify nothing other than a total devotion to human effort.[31]

The model of Christian love which Teilhard takes to be normative is thus not what he understands by the traditional model of Christian love. It is, rather, a model of Christian love which he has himself fashioned out of the gospel notion of *agape* and his own understanding of the needs of evolution. This comes out quite pointedly in the following text: "Nowhere is such a universal love more evident, so it seems to me, than in the charity of the Christian, *such as it is exemplified in the life of a contemporary believer, for whom creation has become newly meaningful in terms of evolution.*"[32] Teilhard's answers have been fashioned out of his own development of Christian theology in such a way that they cohere with a problematic grounded in his own understanding of evolutionary history. To the extent that his own problematic reflects the concerns of others in the contemporary world, and to the extent that his own development of Christian theology is legitimate, to that extent will his apologetic theology be both relevant and Christian.

Summary

The present chapter has been concerned with elucidating Teilhard's apologetic method of correlation in the context of the problem of activating a universal form of love, alone capable of unifying the multiplicity of mankind. For Teilhard such activating power belongs only to Omega. However, the term "Omega" does not possess a univocal meaning in Teilhard's thought; in fact, we have been able to distinguish four senses in which he uses the term. First of all, "Omega" designates the collective unity of mankind upon itself at the end of history. Secondly, "Omega" designates the transcendent, personal Center of this collective unity of mankind. In the third place, "Omega" designates the cosmic Christ, the transcendent personal Center of mankind's unity known through revelation and accepted in faith. And finally, "Omega" designates the Body of Christ, the collective unity of mankind in the cosmic Christ.

The various senses of "Omega" are clearly interrelated inasmuch as each sense represents a further level of analysis which completes the level of analysis which precedes it. However, the various senses of "Omega" are also distinct from one another, and one may feel no compulsion to follow Teilhard from one sense to the next. For example, the Marxist may well feel quite at home with Teilhard's secularist interpretation of "Omega" at the same time that he feels compelled to reject his theistic interpretation of "Omega." Likewise, the theist may be able to accept Teilhard's theistic interpretation without being able to go beyond this point by accepting his christological interpretation. A certain discontinuity exists between the various senses of "Omega" which prevents Teilhard from establishing an absolutely foolproof line of argument which would compel his listener to accept all four senses of the term. In the last analysis, all Teilhard can do is to establish a series of correlative correspondences between the various senses of "Omega," thus inviting his listener to see in each succeeding stage of his argument the legitimate completion of the previous stage. Teilhard would make the Marxist a theist and the theist a Christian, not by asking either to surrender what he already possesses, but rather by asking each to complete what he already possesses in a higher synthesis. In short, Teilhard does not ask his listener to take a road opposite to the one along which he is already traveling, but rather he asks him to follow out the logic of his present commitment so as to move further along the same road.

We may conclude these summary reflections with one observation on the theory of creative union. Because for Teilhard love is the energy of union, love is properly speaking creative, it is the very energy of continuous creation. Moreover, because love, particularly in its universal form, is the work of Christ, Christ's creative function is basically understood by Teilhard in terms of his activating role as the Omega of evolution towards whom the whole of evolution converges and in whom the whole of evolution holds together. In our next chapter we should like to show how Teilhard also attempts to understand the creative function of Christ as the Soul of evolution.

VI

Christ: The Soul of Evolution

Having in the last chapter considered the more important aspects of Teilhard's apologetical method, particularly as these relate to the problem of Omega and the activation of a universal love sufficient to unify the noosphere and thus bring evolution to its successful denouement, we are now in a position to explore the more specifically theological side of Teilhard's effort to understand the relation of Christ to the movement of evolution. However, we intend in the present chapter to limit our investigation of this theme to only those facets of the problem which relate in a direct way to the problem of the one and the many as it is dealt with by Teilhard in the context of the theory of creative union. It is our hope that although confining ourselves to a limited focus of vision, we may nonetheless be able to illuminate several of the areas which we have already discussed, particularly Teilhard's understanding of creation and of the mystical Body in his system.

Mankind: A New Multiplicity to Be Unified

We already noted in Chapter IV that Teilhard sees the appearance of man as the emergence of a new multiplicity which has now to be unified by God's creative action. We also saw that Teilhard envisages the unification of this new multiplicity as coming about through the combined effect of both external and internal forces which may also be considered respectively as passive and active forces of unification from the perspective of the theory of creative union. We further saw that, as the movement of human unification gained momentum, what were originally passively undergone forces of compression and rapprochement, gradually were transformed through the introduction of invention and the rebound effect into actively and purposively controlled media of unification. In other words, at the later stages of human evolution man becomes more and more the master of his own development. This particular train of thought makes of man the architect of his own eventual unity and leads inevitably to the postulation of the unity of mankind as the goal of history. This interpretation of history, however, is corrected by Teilhard in his treatment of universal love as the primary internal force in human unification inasmuch as such a form of love necessitates the further postulation of a present and transcendent personal Center of unity. Hence, God plays an absolutely crucial and indispensable role in the unification of the noosphere.

What appears at the purely phenomenological level of analysis as a process of unification achieved immanently through external and internal forces increasingly controlled by man himself is seen at a deeper level of analysis to involve the energizing activity of God. What initially appeared as a process of self-creation is now seen to be a process involving God's creative activity. If such is the case, how are these two modes of creative activity (the one human and immanent and the other divine and transcendent as well as immanent) to be unified together? If it is not possible to say that man alone creates himself and his future unity or that God alone creates man and man's future unity, how are we to conceive the causality proper to God in this work of creation which is man's unification? We are thus compelled to confront the very problem which Teilhard's phenomenological method habitually eschews, the problem of causality.

The Role of Omega

An initial line of solution to this problem is already offered to us by Teilhard in his analysis of the activating power of Omega as transcendent, personal Center in relation to the problem of love. Man actually unifies the noosphere through his own love, but this love depends upon some superior activating force beyond man. The question is what sort of causality, properly creative in this case, is involved in the activation by this divine Center of a universal form of human love? This question is very difficult to answer for the simple reason that the problem of causality is a properly onto-logical question and Teilhard generally treats the activating power of Omega in largely psychological terms. However, perhaps it is best to avoid making too sharp a dichotomy between ontology and psychology as they meet in personal relationships, and if we do avoid this pitfall, we may be able to reconstruct Teilhard's argu-ment in roughly the following way.

Because Omega, as a transcendent personal Center, is able to function as the collector of human persons beyond the death barrier and thus ensure the irreversibility of the movement of per-sonalization at the heart of evolution, he is thereby able to liberate human action from the impasse which is created by the death barrier itself. Consequently, Omega provides man with a future, the first prerequisite for meaningful activity. In addition to this, Omega, because he is a loving and lovable Center of personalization, gives shape to this future as a locus of enriching possibilities inasmuch as Omega functions as the Center of a community of personalizing interpersonal relationships. In providing man with the possibility of a meaningful personal future, Omega is able to liberate man for love. This is the largely psychological side of Teilhard's argu-ment, but it has ontological consequences. Love, for Teilhard, does not introduce merely accidental changes of no real consequence into humanity; rather, it brings about an ascending growth in being, an ontological enrichment of the person through community rela-tions.

Given the structure of the argument and its orientation towards Omega as the goal of history, it is clear that Teilhard conceives of God's creative activity in terms of final causality, attracting all things upwards into unity like a cosmically powerful magnet. Teil-hard's representation of God's creative causality thus shifts the spotlight away from efficient causality, the mode of causality custo-marily employed to describe God's creative action. This latter notion of creative causality makes good sense if God is understood as an artisan who shaped the creation at some remote point in the past, but as soon as creation is seen to involve a continuous process of unification, other forms of causality become more appropriate to the understanding of this process. God is no longer the Alpha who acted in the past, but the Omega who draws the movement of evolution to its final conclusion by way of activating the unifying power of love. Teilhard's argument, then, resembles Aristotle's argument establishing a First Mover whose mode of causal activity is properly final, although in Aristotle the First Mover operates in the context of a static rather than an evolving universe.[1]

What has been said about the causal relation of Omega theistically interpreted to the movement of evolution, may also be said of Omega christologically interpreted who is able to perform the same functions but with much greater effectiveness. However, the question which must occupy our attention now is not how Omega (or Christ) functions as the transcendent final cause of the evolutionary movement but, rather, how Christ's creative function may be understood in terms of quasi-formal causality.

Mankind: A New Matter in Search of Spirit

If the external and internal forces of unification do in fact correspond to the passive and active relationship of matter and spirit established in the theory of creative union, then, as we observed in Chapter IV, mankind constitutes both the matter and spirit of its own unification, since it both passively undergoes unification as well as actively unites itself. It is particularly the notion of mankind as a new matter (that is a new multiplicity) which we should now like to investigate in Teilhard's early writings in the context of the theory of creative union.

In "La Lutte contre la multitude," Teilhard writes as follows concerning mankind as a new multiplicity:

The human soul is, therefore, eminently spiritual because it is eminently rich with unified multiplicity. In spite of this fact—or rather precisely because of this fact—it does not represent the terminal point of the movement of creation.

Similar in its genesis to all the other forms of monads, man makes his appearance in the world in large numbers. At the beginning, no doubt, mankind was comprised of but a small group of people. However, reproduction was soon able to multiply considerably this rather inauspicious point of departure. Now, it is extremely important that it be clearly understood from the outset that such multiplication was not a mere luxury nor a lucky accident. *The human soul was not made to live alone.*[2] The human monad, just like all the other inferior spheres of the created world, is essentially pluralistic. *By nature*, the reasonable soul is *legion*.

What else can this possibly mean but that the human soul is made for a type of union which simplifies beings at the same time that it appears to complexify them?[3]

In "Mon Univers," an essay devoted to the theory of creative union, Teilhard makes the same point again:

The multiplication of living beings does not represent a return to plurality, but rather the constitution of a multiplicity of a superior order (a new matter) destined to be the support for a new soul. However progressive and spiritualizing it may in fact be, this multiplication is not without danger: for in creating "the mass" it introduces into the world a new possibility (more serious than the preceding) of foolish emancipation and revolt. There is an inherent risk built into being.[4]

A new multiplicity in search of unity, a new matter in search of spirit, a new body in search of a soul. Such is the state of mankind as Teilhard envisions it in these early essays. The dialectic between passivity and activity is at least implied in the way Teilhard has structured the problem, but we see that the stress falls now not on the active role which mankind must play in its own unification, but on its passive position vis-à-vis some principle of unity. Just as the prehominized phase of evolution was characterized by a quest for spirit as the principle of matter's unification, a quest culminating in the appearance of man whose spiritual soul becomes the principle of matter's further unification, so now the hominized phase of evolution is also characterized by a quest for spirit as the principle of mankind's (the new matter) unification, a quest whose goal is as yet unidentified.

Christ: The New Soul of the New Matter

Mankind in its state of multiplicity represents a "flock without a shepherd,"[5] and "all that is needed to reunite and group together the innumerable flock presently dispersed is a very powerful shepherd."[6] There can be no doubt who this shepherd is in Teilhard's mind:

For my own part I accept the reality of the movement which tends to segregate, within the bosom of mankind, a congregation of the faithful dedicated to the great task of "advancing in unity." Moreover, I believe in its truth; I consider the fact that it contains in its ranks a great number of sinners, of the "maimed, the halt, and the blind," to be evidence of this truth. But this does not cause me to believe that the eager multitude crying out today for guidance is in search of any Shepherd other than he who has already brought it bread.

In response to the cry of a world trembling with the desire for unity, and already equipped, through the workings of material progress, with the external links of this unity, Christ is already revealing himself, in the depths of men's hearts, as the Shepherd (the Animator) of the universe.[7]

Jesus is the looked-for Shepherd of the flock of humanity, the Animator of that new matter which is humanity: "I came that they may have life, and have it more abundantly. I am the good shepherd. The good shepherd lays down his life for his sheep . . . and there shall be one fold and one shepherd" (John 10, 10–11. 17). It is the accent on Jesus' role as animator that indicates the direction in which Teilhard is moving in his understanding of the relation of Christ to the universe. Jesus, in his cosmic attributes and functions, is the soul of the evolutionary movement of unification. This emphasis appears already in 1915 in a letter written by Teilhard to his cousin: " 'Natura ingemiscit et parturit,' says St. Paul, more or less. When you suffer and toil, what you are doing is simply attaching your own small effort to him who is the Soul of all creation."[8] Teilhard wishes "to show to those whom the real attracts by its treasures and subjugates with its immanence that the life of the Lord Jesus circulates in all things,—the true Soul of the world."[9] It is the universal Christ who functions like a soul of the universe: "The characteristic attribute of the Universal Element, as it appears to us realized in the figure of Christ, is to be not a quasi-matter, a plastic element, an agent of absorption, but a quasi-Soul, a plasmatic element, a determining force."[10]

While the notion of Christ as the Soul of evolution does not occur as such with great frequency in Teilhard's writings, it does occur with great frequency, and from the very beginning, under a different form: that of the theme of Christ as the *physical* Center of the universe,[11] the term "physical" in this case meaning organic or ontological.[12]

The cosmic Christ is the soul, the physical or organic center, of the evolutionary movement *in toto*, but most particularly of humanity in process of socialization. Because evolution for Teilhard is primarily a movement of unification, and unification is a work which belongs properly to the soul or spirit, it follows logically that in attempting to determine the relationship which obtains between God and the world, Teilhard quite naturally thinks of this relationship in terms of formal, or rather quasi-formal, causality (the causality appropriate to the soul) rather than in terms of efficient causality. A causal relationship of a quasi-formal kind establishes an organic relationship between God in Christ and the world, whereas a causal relationship of an efficient kind seems to Teilhard to establish a relationship which is altogether too extrinsic and hence inadequate to describe the organic kind of unity which Teilhard envisions as being the goal of mankind's thrust towards socialization. Furthermore, inasmuch as evolution for Teilhard is the form assumed for us by God's creative activity, God's creative activity is understood in terms of quasi-formal rather than efficient causality. From being the artisan of a static universe, God becomes in the framework of Teilhard's system the soul of creation as an ongoing process of unification. Or, to put the matter more accurately, *Christ* becomes in the framework of Teilhard's system the soul of creation, the quasi-formal cause of unity. We may now turn to a brief investigation of some of the texts in which Teilhard explicitly underlines the quasi-formal causal role of Christ in creation.

In December of 1918, Teilhard developed an entire essay, entitled "Forma Christi," around this notion of Christ as the quasi-formal cause of creation. In the Introduction to that essay he writes:

More than ever, I think that Christianity is understood by our generation in a manner which is altogether too extrinsic and too narrow. Both in sermons and in the popular imagination, dogma: (1) floats above the universe (without being rooted in it), and (2) appears to be interested in only a *terribly small part* of cosmic reality.[13]

To correct this, "it is necessary to return to the best currents of the Catholic tradition and then to preach a theology in which Christ clearly appears as bound up with the development of the entire universe."[14] How then are we to understand the relationship of Christ to the universe? "Long before the incarnation actually took place (in virtue of a mysterious, but nonetheless revealed, pre-action of the humanity of Jesus), the whole history of the world is constituted by a progressive information of the world by Christ."[15] What then is meant by this term "information":

The term which serves to define the least inadequately the universal influx of Jesus—Center of the world—is "information." Christ unifies his mystical members into a superior finality, order, law of growth, and even sort of consciousness. Christ really *lives* in us. What more can we say than that he really informs us?

In truth, Christ acts on us *like a form. The sum of souls* receptive to this action represents the *matter* which takes shape in him interiorly (substantially).[16]

That Teilhard sees this formal creative causality as being more appropriate to a universe in a state of evolutionary development than efficient creative causality is brought out clearly in a number of texts. The following text from 1953 is characteristic:

Whereas in the case of a static world view, the Creator (conceived of as an efficient cause) remains, whatever may be said to the contrary, *structurally* detached from his work and hence without any easily definable foundation for his immanence; in the case of an evolutionary world view, on the contrary, God can only be conceived of (both structurally and dynamically) in the measure that, like a sort of "formal" cause, he coincides (without being confused) with the Center of convergence of cosmogenesis.[17]

In an essay written in 1918, Teilhard expresses in a particularly clear way his animus against the category of efficient causality:

The term *efficient causality* when applied to *creation* quite accurately affirms the distinction which separates the Creator from his work (i.e. it serves to deny pantheism); however it tells us virtually nothing about the nature of the process which links *participated being* to *uncreated Being*;—on the contrary, it introduces between the two an *exteriority* which is surely exaggerated.[18]

If the notion of efficient causality adequately safeguards the contingency of the universe and the transcendence of God and accurately describes God's creative action considered as an isolated act in the remote past establishing a fundamentally static universe, it is incapable of giving expression to God's involvement and immanence in a creation conceived of as an ongoing process. If the notion of final causality adequately underlines the fact that God is the goal and hence magnetic pole of the movement of creation, it also fails to illuminate satisfactorily the actual modality of God's creative activity within the ongoing process.[19] What is needed is a notion which goes beyond creative action (linked as it is to efficient causality). What is needed is a notion like creative union, for God creates by uniting, not extrinsically but immanently. The proper mode of God's creative action is quasi-formal, for he is the soul (or quasi-soul) of evolution, since the essential function of the soul is to unite.

The reason why Teilhard insists on the fact that God acts upon the creation in a *quasi*-formal mode of causality, as *a sort* of soul, is not difficult to discern, for if he did not, his position would fall into pantheism. The term "quasi" is used by Teilhard, then, to safguard the transcendence of God vis-à-vis his creation; but it is also used to safeguard the integrity of the creation itself as well. To underline this latter fact Teilhard coined the expression "l'union différencie," which in its broadest acceptation may be translated as "union differentiates," but which is more aptly translated as "union personalizes" in the context of its more usual reference to the relationship between God and mankind. God's quasi-formal relationship to mankind not only does not destroy personhood, but actually enhances it and brings it to fulfillment. Such is the intent of the formula *"l'union différencie."* As such, the formula begins to appear with regularity only in the mid-thirties,[20] but its components and thought content are visible from the earliest essays.[21]

The Mystical Body of Christ

If the theme of Christ as the Soul of creation bulks rather large in Teilhard's early writings, it is because the notion of the mystical Body also plays a pivotal role in the development of Teilhard's thought. We have already seen that Teilhard seeks to develop ecclesiological doctrine in the direction of an understanding of the Church which would emphasize its role in the progress of evolution as a phylum of love whose function it is to generate that universal form necessary to the total unification of the noosphere. The emphasis on the Church as the mystical Body of Christ involves an attempt on Teilhard's part to develop ecclesiological doctrine away from juridical categories in the direction of organic categories.

For Teilhard there exists no opposition between these two emphases on love and organicity, inasmuch as love plays a properly organic role in unifying the members of the Body of Christ.[22] Love relates the members of Christ, not tangentially or extrinsically, but radially, center to center, making them one Body, animated by one common Presence. It is this understanding of the Church as an organism of persons united together in Christ through love which Teilhard is seeking to promote. What is the relation between this understanding of the Church and Teilhard's theory of creative union? According to Teilhard himself, the relation between the two is very close:

The reader will have already observed for himself that the philosophy of creative union is nothing more than the development, the generalization, the extension to the entire universe of what the Church teaches us concerning the growth of Christ. *It is the philosophy of the universe conceived in function of the notion of the mystical Body.* It was in reflecting upon the mystical Body that I discovered the theory of creative union and it is only by keeping the connection between the two in mind that one can hope to understand the theory of creative union: it is only by seeking to love and to see Christ everywhere that one will come to understanding.[23]

Seven years later, Teilhard writes:

I would like to show in this chapter that Christianity so assumes its full significance in function of the theory of creative union that this theory, instead of being regarded as a philosophical point of view confirmed and brought to fulfillment by the Christian point of view, would rather merit being called a philosophical extension of faith in the incarnation.[24]

Inspired by his own personal meditations on the notion of the mystical Body, Teilhard's theory of creative union is an attempt to extend this notion beyond the frontiers of the Church as such so as to include the whole of the cosmos. The theory of creative union, then, envisages something larger than the mystical Body, or to put the point more accurately, it envisages a cosmic Body of Christ whose axis is the mystical Body of Christ. Through the interaction of these notions, cosmogenesis becomes for Teilhard, in the final analysis, a process of christogenesis, the building up of the Body of Christ. Beginning with the notion of Christ as the Soul of the mystical Body, Teilhard extends this notion in such a way that Christ becomes the Soul of the cosmic Body as well.[25]

It is perhaps worth noting at this point what seems to be a rather curious aspect of Teilhard's doctrine of the quasi-formal causality of Christ in relation to his mystical Body and to his cosmic Body as well. The notion of a Soul of the mystical Body is by no means untraditional in Catholic ecclesiology. What is rather unusual, however, is the fact that Teilhard links the notion to Christ himself rather than to the Holy Spirit, who is traditionally considered to be the Soul of the mystical Body, the bond of love in the Church as he is the bond of love in the Trinity. The Christian doctrine of the Holy Spirit is never really explored by Teilhard in the framework of his evolutionary world view, and he appears to have remained content with simply transferring to Christ functions traditionally attributed to the Holy Spirit. Given the fact that Teilhard habitually experienced Christ in terms of his spiritual omnipresence to the universe, little room is left for him to develop a pneumatology as distinct from a christology, and hence his natural proclivity to identify the two areas.

The Pleroma

Teilhard's notion of the cosmic Body of Christ corresponds, at least in Teilhard's own mind, to what Paul calls the "pleroma." For Teilhard, the pleroma constitutes the synthesis of Christ and all created things, and it is through this synthesis that all things are created because it is in Christ that all things are unified together.[26]

Writing in 1945, Teilhard links together the mysteries of creation, incarnation, and redemption with the notion of pleromization: "Seen in this light, the three mysteries of creation, incarnation, and redemption, become in truth, in the context of a renewed Christology, but three aspects of one and the same fundamental process, which we may term the 'mystery of the creative union of the world in God' or 'pleromization.' "[27] It would be difficult to exaggerate the importance of this text for our understanding of the theory of creative union. The pleroma for Teilhard represents the cosmos in a state of completion through its final unification in God (or Christ, "the active center, the living link, the organizing soul of the pleroma").[28] Pleromization, then, represents the process of unification taking place in history which leads to this state of completion. Hence, pleromization is equivalent to creative union, and the pleroma represents the completed state of both. As Christopher Mooney observes: " 'Creative union,' 'Pleromization,' 'Christogenesis,' are therefore synonymous terms to describe the exercise of Christ's power as organic Center of the universe, a continuous influence which is both creative, unitive, and redemptive, and which results in his Plenitude at the Parousia."[29]

In 1946, Teilhard offers us one of his most carefully nuanced statements regarding the structure of the pleroma and of the process of pleromization leading to it:

A final and supreme definition of point Omega: a focus which is at one and the same time one and yet complex, in which, cemented together by the person of Christ, are to be found three concentric centers, each more profound than the preceding; exteriorly, the immanent ("natural") summit of the humano-cosmic cone; located further within, at the middle, the immanent ("supernatural") summit of the "ecclesiastical" or christic cone; and, right at the heart, finally, the transcendent trinitarian and divine center. This is the complete pleroma joined together through the mediatory action of Christ-Omega.[30]

Teilhard here indicates that the union of God with the world involves a complex process of mediation beginning with the overarching mediational function of Christ vis-à-vis the Trinity and the world. Christ's mediational function is in turn further mediated through the relationship of the Church to humanity and the relationship of humanity to the material world. As man transforms the material world, so Christ through his Church transforms man and with him the material world as well. Teilhard is able to distinguish the various lines of mediation linking the cosmos to God, but he is quite incapable of separating them and thus rupturing the lines of connection which tie the entire cosmos together in God.

Teilhard's view of the relationship between God and the cosmos rests upon a simple and yet complex insight into what might be termed a process of progressive incorporation, each stage of the evolutionary process being successively incorporated into a higher stage through the introduction of a new principle of unity and hence of transformation. Teilhard does not in fact confuse together the various levels of reality so as to achieve a monistic pantheism in which everything is simply identified together. Rather, Teilhard's system might better be characterized as a pantheism of union in which the various levels of reality are synthesized and at the same time differentiated, in this way being brought to fulfillment. Each stage of the evolutionary process is a questing after the stage which is to follow, for the completion of the one stage depends upon the appearance of the next stage. But the process as a whole is awaiting the pleroma in which God will be all in all and the all will find its completion in the One. At this point, creation will have attained its goal, for it will have attained its maximum point of union. The many will have become one in the One.

The question, however, remains: if the many find completion through union with the One, does the One also find some sort of completion through its union with the many? Does the creation, in short, add anything to God?

The Completion of the One

This problem fascinated Teilhard from the very beginning of his literary career right up to the time of his death. Christopher Mooney takes the following approach to Teilhard's treatment of the problem:

The assertion that the world's movement towards unity "completes" God in some way is unusual and needs to be clarified. Again it must be kept in mind that Teilhard is referring always to the building up of the Body of Christ in the present supernatural order.

Teilhard is doing nothing more nor less than simply asserting in an evolutionary context the paradox which is already contained in St. Paul: the Pleroma of Christ cannot constitute an intrinsic completion of God himself, but it will nonetheless in some sense be a real completion. But why go to such lengths to insist on the second half of the paradox? The answer is that Teilhard wants to do away once and for all with the idea that God's continuous act of creation is one of *absolute* gratuity.[31]

The theme of God's completion is developed by Teilhard in conjunction with two other aspects of his system: the first is the doctrine of the mystical Body and the second is the problem of the gratuity of creation. Father Mooney's commentary notes both these aspects and rightly insists on the contextual background of the mystical Body and the fact that Teilhard is attempting to eliminate any hint of creation being an arbitrary act on God's part. Basic to both these aspects of the question, however, is the fundamental problematic out of which the whole thematic of completion arises: the question of activating action. Unless man can become convinced that his efforts contribute to a work which is irreversible in character and hence absolutely meaningful both to himself and to God, he cannot be properly motivated to make the sacrifices necessary for the completion of this work. Teilhard wishes to make it abundantly clear that, since the work of creation leading to the pleroma is a cooperative venture between God and man, both parties are absolutely interested in its success because both parties have something to gain from the successful outcome to creation. Furthermore, if man's achievement remains somehow extrinsic to God, not really affecting him and hence not really mattering to him, then this achievement loses its absoluteness, partaking as it then would of that absolute contingency which Teilhard is trying to destroy.

Teilhard's attempt to ground the motivation of God's creative activity in some complementing (or completing) gain which would accrue to God in the pleroma underscores once again his uneasiness with the traditional notion that love is the only motive of creation. We have already discussed this issue in Chapter I and may now complete our survey with the two following texts:

Are creation, incarnation, and redemption not three acts indissolubly linked together in the appearance of participated being even if each marks a further stage in the gratuity of the divine operation? And does not the appearance of participated being itself respond to some more well-defined need than the simple emotion of a *Bonum diffusivum sui?*[32]

The Scholastics quite rightly tell us that "God creates through love." But what kind of love is this, which proves to be inexplicable with respect to its subject and humiliating with respect to its object, and *which is not founded upon some need* (unless it be the pleasure to be found in giving for giving's sake)?[33]

These two texts bear comparison with a rather revealing observation made by Teilhard in a letter written to Bruno de Solages in 1935:

In order to save one aspect of God, we have to say that "God could not have created." However, I am even more struck by the necessity we feel under also to say (in order to save another aspect of God) that God had to create so as to complete himself in something exterior to himself. An *absolutely free* creation seems to me patently absurd (and extremely difficult to reconcile with the existence and importance of the creation-incarnation-redemption).[34]

Teilhard does not deny that God creates out of love, but he seems to believe that if one insists on love as the only motive of creation, then one automatically has to think of creation as an arbitrary act. It is likely that Teilhard was himself exposed to a kind of theology which seemed to him to maintain such an equivalency between love and arbitrary gratuity. However, instead of attempting to rectify the false understanding of love which lies at the root of this equation, Teilhard prefers to further guarantee God's commitment by seeking out some need in God which provides him with an additional motive to create. Teilhard consistently tries to qualify this need in such a way that God is not made out to be imperfect and hence lacking something with which creation will supply him. However, it is hard to avoid the conclusion that beneath all the qualifications there remains a residual lack in God which is completed by the creation. Teilhard maintains that this need or lack does not lie in the area of God's being but only in the area of his act of union. What precisely this distinction is meant to convey is difficult to determine.

By way of concluding this discussion on the theme of completion in Teilhard's system, we begin by making two observations. First, to the extent that this theme is connected with the theme of the building up of the Body of Christ, it is perfectly traditional and also coheres perfectly well with the totality of Teilhard's system. Secondly, to the extent that this theme is caught up in a faulty understanding of God's love as the motive of creation, it appears to constitute an unnecessary rationalizing of the doctrine of creation.

Given the centrality of love in Teilhard's total system, there seems to be no really cogent reason why Teilhard should shy away from affirming with all possible emphasis the centrality of love in God's creative activity. In fact, for Teilhard the very dynamism of creation depends upon God's being both loving and lovable, as we saw in the preceding chapter. However, in attempting to secure God's absolute involvement in creation, Teilhard draws back from the simple and unequivocal affirmation that love alone guarantees that involvement. Undoubtedly, his theological formation at the beginning of this century is largely to blame for his difficulties at this point.

Teilhard rightly emphasizes the fact that in the present economy of creation and salvation God needs man for the completion of his creative and redemptive design. The Body of Christ, which is the goal of creation, can only be built up into its plenitude through the collaboration of the divine and the human together. In this sense, then, man's activity really does complete the deepest intentions of God's love by bringing the creation to its fulfillment. And certainly in this sense man does something for God which God, precisely because of his love for man, cannot do for himself. Man, then, completes the yearning of God's own love for man and his desire for man's salvation, which consists in man's union with God. Keeping in mind the dangers of excessive anthropomorphism at this point, we may therefore say that man completes God's love for the creation by bringing that love to the effective realization of its goal, which is the good of the creation.

Through such a line of reasoning we arrive at the paradoxical position that God is completed through creation because the creation is completed. And it is this completion of creation alone which God has in view in creating. The completion of creation serves to complete the disinterested *agape*-love of God for creation, and hence in this sense God is also completed through the completion of his creatures. While such a love is mysterious, it is not irrational or arbitrary. On the contrary, it is selfishness which is irrational and arbitrary in its activity; it is selfishness which cannot be depended upon. Creation matters infinitely to God *because of* his love, not *in spite of* it. It matters to him infinitely precisely because he loves it as a reality in and for itself and not as a reality which he must exploit for his own gain.

We may conclude, then, that Teilhard's notion that the creation completes God can be understood in an acceptable sense, but not in the sense that creation supplies God with something which he lacks, and hence that he creates in order to gain what is wanting to him. Teilhard both endorses and seeks to avoid endorsing this latter unacceptable sense of the term "completion." Having explored Teilhard's understanding of the completive effect of the pleroma vis-à-vis God, we must now turn our attention to Teilhard's understanding of the pleroma vis-à-vis the traditional doctrine of hell.

Final Apocatastasis?

Given Teilhard's overarching concern for unity, it would be logical enough to assume that Teilhard's system ends on a note of pleromic unity in which nothing is lost. However, Teilhard's attitude to the traditional doctrine of hell is somewhat more complex than simple rejection. In point of fact, during the years preceding the writing of *The Divine Milieu*, he quite unambiguously affirms the existence and necessity of hell.[35] In *The Divine Milieu* itself we note for the first time a considerable conflict in Teilhard's mind between his faith in the existence of hell and a personal reluctance to accept the fact that anyone is actually damned:

You have told me, O God, to believe in hell. But you have forbidden me to hold with absolute certainty that any single man has been damned. I shall therefore make no attempt to consider the damned here, nor even to discover—by whatsoever means—whether there are any. I shall accept the existence of hell on your word, *as a structural element in the universe*, and I shall pray and meditate until this awe-inspiring thing appears to me as a strengthening and even blessed complement to the vision of your omnipresence which you have opened out to me.[36]

Having discussed the place which hell occupies as a complement to the Pleroma, Teilhard then ends with this prayer:

I pray, O Master, that the flames of hell may not touch me nor any of those whom I love, and even that they may not touch anyone (I know, my God, that you will forgive this bold prayer); but that, for each and every one of us, their somber glow may add, together with all the abysses that they reveal, to the blazing plentitude of the divine *milieu*.[37]

The desires and doubts expressed in these texts hardly amount to a denial of the traditional doctrine but, rather, serve to express a certain tension in Teilhard's mind.

In 1944, Teilhard returns for the last time to an explicit treatment of the doctrine of hell as such. It is worth quoting a rather long text in full because it summarizes the development of more than a quarter of a century of reflection on Teilhard's part.

The existence of a hell is, together with the mystery of the cross, one of the most disconcerting and most criticized aspects of the Christian faith. And yet, reduced to its essence, nothing could be more in con-

5

formity with the perspectives of an evolutionary world view than this dogma. All evolution (at least within the limit of our experience) involves selection and failure. Hence it is impossible for us to imagine in the context of the totality of the process the unification of the world in God without making some room (*de jure* if not *de facto*) for that which would eventually escape from such a beatifying process. Could the saving operation in which creation consists be expected to yield a one hundred per cent return? Christianity does not decide the issue one way or the other, but it does not absolutely deny such a possibility. It does, however, remind us that there can be loss—and that, in this case, the "condemned" elements would be eliminated forever, that is rejected to the antipodes of God.

From this point of view, to posit the existence of a hell is simply a negative way of affirming that man can only find, with absolute physical and organic necessity, his happiness and fulfillment by reaching the terminus of his evolution through fidelity to the movement in which he is involved. Supreme life (that is a full awareness of all in all) or supreme death (that is an awareness of an infinitely disunited kind). Everything or nothing. This is the alternative with which we are faced by the existence of hell, and it is this alternative which the notion of hell seeks to translate into intelligible terms for us. Who would dare to say that this condition does not harmonize well with what we know and all that we feel? And who would dare to say that such a conception fails to do justice to the importance of life and the dignity of man?

Having admitted this much, let us not attempt to go any further than this; that is let us avoid getting ourselves involved in fallacious attempts to represent or imagine what hell is like. It cannot be reiterated often enough that hell is known to us and holds meaning for us only to the extent that it is seen to be but the inversion of heaven, the pole opposite God. Which amounts to saying that it can only be defined negatively in relation to the heaven which it is not. Every effort to "reify" and describe it in itself, like any other isolated entity, runs the risk of leading us (as we have only too often seen) into absurd and detestable positions.

In summary, then, hell is an "indirect" reality, which we may well experience quite intensely, but which it is neither profitable nor possible to perceive or to consider directly—exactly like the case of the mountain climber who is fully aware that beneath him gapes an abyss and whose essential task is to turn his back on it.

I would not be so temerarious as to say the views proposed here are as yet commonly admitted by Christian theologians. But, in any case, they do represent the point of view which is now gaining ground and becoming established in Christian practice. And hence this point of

view has a very good chance of giving expression to the living orthodoxy of tomorrow.[38]

While refusing to speculate on whether or not anyone is actually
in hell (as in *The Divine Milieu*), Teilhard reëmphasizes the directional character of evolution as a movement both towards unity
and towards multiplicity by stressing the alternatives available to
human freedom. This line of approach is particularly prominent
in the early essays as well. If the freedom of man is crucial to the
eventual success of evolution and at least posits the possibility of
a hell, Teilhard refuses to allow that it can in the end prevent the
successful outcome of the thrust of evolution towards final synthesis.

Teilhard never loses sight of the fact that "the right outcome" of
evolution is one thing, while that of the individual quite another.
Ultimate victory for humanity through union with Omega does not
mean personal victory for each human being.[39]

While this is undoubtedly true, it needs to be balanced in good
dialectical fashion by the affirmation that universal salvation is at
least a possibility. Such is apparently Teilhard's intention at any
rate.

Summary

By way of concluding this chapter we may just briefly summarize
the results of our investigation into Teilhard's understanding of
Christ's quasi-formal creative causality. Beginning with the notion
that humanity constitutes a new matter, a new multiplicity, to be
unified by a new Soul, Teilhard finds this new Soul of mankind in
Christ who acts as the principle of unity of a new Body. This Body
possesses not only an ecclesial dimension but also a cosmic dimension and thus includes not only the whole of mankind but also
the whole of the cosmos as well. Teilhard's understanding of Christ's
quasi-formal creative relation to the entire evolutionary movement
constitutes an extension and transposition of the traditional notion
that the Holy Spirit functions as the unifying soul of the mystical
Body. While Teilhard does not simply identify Christ and the
Spirit, he easily transfers to Christ functions traditionally appro-
priated to the Spirit. Because Teilhard habitually thinks of Christ
in terms of his risen state and his cosmic omnipresence, he really

has no room to develop a pneumatology as distinct from a christology and hence identifies the two areas for the most part.

We also discussed Teilhard's use of the formula *"l'union différencie"* to underscore the fact that Christ's quasi-formal presence and
causality do not destroy the personhood of the creatures but rather
enhance it and bring it to fulfillment. We further tried to assess
Teilhard's view that the many have some sort of completive effect
vis-à-vis the One. We concluded that the theme of completion is
perfectly valid in the context of the notion of the building up of
the Body of Christ, which is the usual context in which Teilhard
employs it, and that it even has validity in relation to God himself
if it is understood in rigorous connection with the doctrine of God's
love as the motive of creation. Unfortunately, Teilhard found it
personally difficult to maintain this rigorous connection and hence
veered off into what at least tends to be a rationalization of the
mystery. And finally, we looked at the development of Teilhard's
thinking on the doctrine of hell, concluding that he does not hold
an explicit doctrine of final apocatastasis even if his refusal after
1927 to speculate on whether anyone is in fact in hell leaves this
possibility open.

Having looked at the main lines of Teilhard's system in the
context of the problem of the one and the many and his theory
of creative union, it remains for us in our final chapter to explore
the implications of this system for spirituality—the spirituality of
creative union.

VII

The Spirituality of Creative Union

The spirituality of Teilhard, the spirituality lived by him personally with intense conviction and promoted by him for the sake of the Christian in the modern world,

is at once the crown of his thought and one of the most powerful motivations of his scientific and philosophical endeavor. In Teilhard's own eyes, the most important fruit of his own thinking and reflection was a new stress on certain aspects of the Christian life and a consequent renewal in the area of spirituality. Without doubt this was the principal message Teilhard believed he must mediate to his fellow men and fellow Catholics.[1]

To neglect this dimension of Teilhard's work, then, would be to pass over an integral part of the man himself and also of his theory of creative union.

In this chapter, we should like to show how Teilhardian spirituality coheres with the emphases of the theory of creative union which we have investigated in the preceding chapters. In particular, we should like to show how Teilhardian spirituality is a spirituality of the divine milieu; a spirituality devoted to the building up of the Body of Christ through both activity and passivity; a spirituality profoundly rooted in the eucharistic celebration, the sacrament of unity; and finally, a spirituality committed to the unification of both the person and the total human community through purity and charity. We should also like to show that, as Teilhard himself says in *The Divine Milieu*, "the sojourner in the divine milieu is not a pantheist," but that nonetheless "Christianity alone saves . . . the essential aspiration of all mysticism: *to be united* (i.e. to become the other) *while remaining oneself*."[2] We therefore turn now to Teilhard's spirituality, the spirituality of creative union, a spirituality devoted to the resolution in life of the problem of the one and the many.

The Divine Milieu

Although Teilhard developed an entire book around the notion of the divine milieu, it may not be clear, even to the reader of that volume, just exactly what Teilhard means by the expression. Hence our initial question must be: what precisely is this divine milieu of which Teilhard speaks? While this notion appears in its most elaborated form in the work of the same name written in the winter of 1926–1927, it is a notion which has a prior history in Teilhard's writings. In fact, it is already discernible in "La Vie cosmique," an essay written in 1916.[3] In "La Lutte contre la multitude," written one year later, the term "divine milieu" itself appears.[4] A few months later, Teilhard devoted an entire essay to this theme, but under the title of "Le Milieu mystique," an expression which is equivalent to the term "divine milieu." The mystical milieu represents for Teilhard nothing other than the mystical Body of Christ, whose Center is Christ and whose Body is constituted by mankind. It is both a divine and human synthesis, whose final consummation depends upon both divine and human collaboration.[5] But the mystical milieu in actuality is even broader in extension than the mystical Body as such, for it also includes the cosmic Body of Christ, as Teilhard notes explicitly at the end of 1917 in "L'Union créatrice."[6]

In seeking to delineate the nature of the divine milieu in *The Divine Milieu* itself, Teilhard draws all the threads of his previous reflection into a single paragraph:

The divine milieu henceforward assumes for us the savor and specific features which we were looking for. In it we recognize an omnipresence which acts upon us by assimilating us into itself, *in unitate Corporis Christi*. As a consequence of the Incarnation, the divine immensity has transformed itself for us into *the omnipresence of christification*. All the good that I can do, *opus et operatio*, is physically gathered in, by something of itself, into the reality of the consummated Christ. Everything I endure, with faith and love, by way of diminishment or death, makes me a little more closely an integral part of his mystical Body. Quite specifically, it is *Christ whom we make or whom we undergo in all things.* Not only *diligentibus omnia convertuntur in bonum,* but, more clearly still, *convertuntur in Deum* and, quite explicitly, *convertuntur in Christum.*[7]

It is within the overarching, vivifying context of the divine milieu, the Body of Christ, that creative union actually occurs, for it is within the divine milieu that God in Christ acts upon the whole movement of evolution as the quasi-formal unifying Center of ultimate synthesis. It is within the divine milieu that all things are created by being both unified and transformed. It is, thus, within the divine milieu that the spirituality of creative union becomes operative. In fact, Teilhard indicates in the text we have just cited one of the focal emphases of this spirituality: the dialectic between what we do and what we undergo, the dialectic between activity and passivity.

Activity and Passivity

Just as the notion of the divine milieu had developed for slightly more than a decade before coming to full bloom in *The Divine Milieu,*[8] so too the theme of activity and passivity, which bulks so large in that work, also had developed from the seeds of the earliest essays. Teilhard had so assimilated this aspect of his spirituality personally that he was able to write as early as 1918 that

this point of view of human activity and passivity, integrally sanctified and divinized, has become so familiar to me that I am able to live it in practice without the slightest effort. I find in this point of view an ease and freedom of movement, a clarity of judgment and decision, which make me intensely desire that many others should understand and adopt the same position.[9]

That this doctrine is intimately connected with the Christian's union with Christ in the mystical Body is underscored in the same essay: "Really, literally, in the hypothesis of Christ adopting and supernaturalizing the natural evolution of the world, *quidquid patimur, Christus agit* and *quidquid agimus, Christus agitur.*"[10]

Whatever we undergo is done by Christ, and whatever we do is done to Christ. Whatever we undergo or do contributes to the building up of Christ's Body whose members we are. "Whether he lives or dies, *through* his life and *through* his death, the Christian in some sense completes his God."[11] All our activities and passivities become sanctified in the divine milieu where we live in continual contact with Christ and with one another.

In 1924 Teilhard explicitly relates the theme of activity and passivity to the theory of creative union:

From the point of view of creative union, the law and ideal of all goodness (moral as well as physical) come to expression in one single rule (which is also a hope for the future): "in everything, promote and undergo the unity of the world." Promote it inasmuch as it has need of the cooperation of the elements in order to be consummated. Undergo it inasmuch as its realization is primarily the effect of a synthetic domination, superior to our own effort. Confirmed, defined, and transfigured through faith in the Incarnation, this rule of action assumes an incomparable urgency and satisfaction. It can also be easily translated into a number of immediately practical duties. We are going to see that for the Christian committed to the unification of the world in Christ, the work of the interior life, both in its moral and mystical dimensions, can be entirely reduced to two essential and complementary movements: to conquer the world on the one hand, and to escape from it on the other. These two movements arise quite naturally out of one another and represent the two conjoined forms of the very same tendency: to be united with God through the world.[12]

The spirituality of the Christian is essentially a spirituality of unification; in everything, he is committed to promoting or undergoing unity. Nothing, save sin which promotes disunity, is excluded from the task of building up the Body of Christ. Both activity and passivity play their own appropriate roles in the work of creation which is achieved through their combination.

We may just recall at this point the fact that Teilhard also uses the dialectic between activity and passivity to describe the relationship between matter and spirit. This is most clearly underlined in a text which we have previously cited:

For the elements grouped together by the soul into a body (and by that very fact elevated to a superior degree of being) "*plus esse est plus cum pluribus uniri.*" For the soul itself, the principle of unity, "*plus esse est plus plura unire.*" For both the soul and the body, to receive or communicate union, is to undergo the creative influence of God "*qui creat uniendo.*"[13]

Transposing this statement into our present context, we may say that whether man promotes the movement of unification of the cosmos through his activity or undergoes it through his passive receptivity, in either case he "undergoes the creative influence of God '*qui creat uniendo.*' " In the context of socialization, man is neither spirit alone (that is the principle of unification) nor matter alone (that is that which is unified), but rather he is both. And hence he must both unify and be unified. However, in either case he is created through the quasi-formal creative causality of Christ, the soul of evolution. Whether we act or suffer, whether we give or receive, we are further incorporated into the Body of Christ which is the locus of God's creative action.

Furthermore, through activity and passivity the Christian becomes simultaneously attached to and detached from the world, for he must at one and the same time be in the world without being of it. Only love is able to sustain such a dialectical relationship to the world because only love is able to attach us permanently to the other as other and in this way to detach (or ex-centrate) us from ourselves. Detachment no longer involves for Teilhard a withdrawal from the world, but rather a withdrawal from selfishness. Detachment is a way of being in the world for the world (that is for other persons) rather than for the egocentric self. Attachment to the world leads to a detachment from the self which alone permits an authentically Christian attachment. To be of the world is to be *conformed* to the *status quo* of a world that is passing away, to exist in an exploitative relationship of pleasure-seeking and selfishness to the world. To be in the world is to *transform* the *status quo* of a world that has an eschatological appointment, to exist in a relationship of active hope to the future of the world in God.

If attachment and detachment are thus to be considered as modalities of love, so too are activity and passivity. Love is gift, but it is not simply the gift of the self to the other. It is also openness to and reception of the gift of the other. Love is both giving and receiving, enriching and being enriched, attachment to the other and detachment from the self. It comes as no surprise that the spirituality of creative union turns out to be a spirituality of love, for love-energy is the very energy of unification and union. We shall have occasion to reiterate this point again in this chapter, but for the moment we wish to follow the theme of activity and passivity as it relates to the problem of nature and grace in the context of spirituality.

Nature and the Supernatural in the Context of Spirituality

The purpose of the phase of action is to construct a natural pleni-tude which may subsequently be transformed in and by Christ into the supernatural plenitude of the pleroma. The phase of passivity, if understood to some extent at least as the phase of receptivity to the divine transforming action, underscores the element of discon-tinuity between our own activity and the building up of the Body of Christ as a supernatural, organic reality. Or to state the same point in other terms, our natural human activity is preparatory to the establishment of the Kingdom of God, but it cannot of and by itself bring in the Kingdom. Teilhard does not obliterate the dis-tinction between nature and the supernatural but, rather, notes both the continuity and discontinuity between them by indicating the importance of a creative transformation which elevates one stage to a higher one.

The Christian is not in the world in order to be *conformed* to it but to *transform* it in Christ and thus bring it to fulfillment. The Christian must be in the world, through immersion in the phase of attachment and action, in order to unify it immanently according to the law of incarnation. But he must also simultaneously refuse to be of the world, through emergence in the phase of detachment and passivity, lest it be forgotten that the final unity of the world will be achieved only by means of a transformation dependent upon the parousia of Christ. It would be as much a mistake for the Christian to seek only the supernatural unity of the world as it is for the secularist to seek only the natural unity of the world. These two unities are related to one another as preparation to fulfillment, and it is the task of the Christian to synthesize the discontinuous continuity between them through his spirituality.

It has more than once been argued that the central problem in

Teilhard's thought and spirituality is the relationship between God and the world. N. M. Wildiers, for example, makes this point with great emphasis:

The problem of the relationship between God and the universe is in fact the central problem of the spiritual life of Teilhard de Chardin. It is only from this point of view that one can hope to grasp the unity and coherence of his immense output of writings. This initial problem constitutes the point of departure of all the important themes which he treated in his writings.

However, the problem of the relationship between God and the world was for him more than a purely abstract and theoretical problem which could be calmly discussed at academic conferences or in dry as dust treatises. This question of the relationship between the historical and the transcendent constituted for him as for Hegel a really existential problem in which he was engaged with his whole being as if it was a matter of his very existence as a man and as a Christian.[14]

Teilhard wished to address both the secular humanist and the Christian, inviting the former to see in Christianity the means of consummating the unity of the natural world in a higher, transcendent unity, and inviting the latter to see in commitment to the world the indispensable means of preparing for that superior consummation.

Much like Paul Tillich,[15] Teilhard considered himself to be living constantly in a boundary situation, on the boundary where the Church and the world meet for dialogue and, it is hoped, for synthesis. In his largely apologetical and autobiographical essay of 1934, entitled "Comment je crois," Teilhard describes this boundary situation as follows:

The originality of my belief consists in the fact that it is rooted in two domains of life usually considered to be antagonistic to one another. Through my education and intellectual formation, I belong to the "children of heaven." However, by temperament and owing to my professional studies I am "a child of the earth." As a result, situated as I am by circumstances at the heart of two worlds with whose theoretical positions, language, and sentiments I am well acquainted through long experience, I have not tried to erect any walls between these two areas in my own interior life. Rather, I have allowed both these apparently contradictory influences to react on one another with complete freedom in the depths of myself. Now, at the terminus of this operation, after thirty years consecrated to the pursuit of interior unity, I have the impression that a synthesis has taken place quite naturally between these two currents which attract me. And I have found that far from one destroying the other, both have served mutually to reinforce one another. Today, I probably believe more in God than ever—and I certainly believe more than ever in the world. Do we not perhaps find here, in terms of the life of a single individual, at least in outline form, the particular solution of the overarching spiritual problem which at the present moment so troubles the advance guard of a humanity on the march?[16]

Teilhard's attempt to synthesize activity and passivity, and attachment and detachment, within the context of a vital contemporary Christian spirituality is, then, simply an aspect of a larger, more all-encompassing effort to synthesize without confusion God and the world, the supernatural and the natural, religion and scientific humanism. And while Teilhard does refer to activity and passivity as phases, which might tend to suggest that they follow one another in distinct succession, it is clear that his real intention is to show that they are actually only distinguishable aspects of one and the same process which is taking place continually and simultaneously.

To sum up the results of our investigation thus far, we may say that the spirituality of creative union is a spirituality lived always within the ambiance of the divine milieu or the Body of Christ in both its mystical or ecclesial dimension (the Church) and its cosmic extension (the world). It is a spirituality of both activity and passivity, of attachment and detachment; a spirituality of love synthesizing in a discontinuous continuity the order of nature and the order of the supernatural. It is a spirituality of unification whose goal is the establishment of the pleroma. It is also a spirituality rooted in the sacramental life of the Church, particularly the sacrament of the Eucharist, the sacrament of unity par excellence.

The Eucharist

The Eucharist is considered in the context of virtually all the themes which we have already discussed and occupies an absolutely central place in both Teilhard's thought and spirituality. In fact, perhaps no other theme better illustrates the unity between Teilhard the thinker and Teilhard the priest of God.

However, just as Teilhard is unable to think in terms of the mystical Body without at the same time extending this doctrine of Catholic faith to embrace a cosmic Body as well, he is unable to think of the eucharistic consecration of the bread and the wine without at the same time extending it to encompass the consecration of the cosmos as well. This accent is already discernible as early as 1918.

When Christ, extending the movement of his Incarnation, descends upon the bread to replace it, his action is not limited to the material parcel which his presence for a moment volatilizes.

Rather, the transubstantiation extends to a real, if attenuated, divinization of the whole universe.

From the cosmic element into which he has inserted himself, the Word acts to subjugate and assimilate to himself all the rest of the cosmos.[17]

In 1916 Teilhard had asked, "besides communion with God and communion with the earth, is there also communion with God through the earth—the earth becoming like a great host in which God would be contained for us?"[18] Indeed, as we have seen, the earth is a great host for Teilhard. Or to be more precise, our activities constitute the bread and our sufferings the wine which is offered to God on the cosmic altar of the world, awaiting the words of consecration and transformation.

Receive, O Lord, this all-embracing host which your whole creation, moved by your magnetism, offers you this dawn of a new day. This bread, our toil, is of itself, I know, but an immense fragmentation; this wine our pain, is no more, I know, than a draught which dissolves. Yet in the very depths of this formless mass you have implanted—and this I am sure of, for I feel it—an irresistible and sanctifying desire which makes us cry out, believer and unbeliever alike: "Lord, make us one!"[19]

This is Teilhard's Mass on the altar of the world which he said so frequently during his lifetime when deprived by his circumstances of the opportunity actually to celebrate.

In August of 1923, he writes to his cousin regarding this Mass, emphasizing the same point which we have just quoted:

I keep developing, and slightly improving, with the help of prayer, my "Mass upon things." It seems to me that in a sense the true substance to be consecrated each day is the world's development during that day—the bread symbolizing appropriately what creation succeeds in producing, the wine (blood) what creation causes to be lost in exhaustion and suffering in the course of its effort.[20]

The theme of activity and passivity is thus effectively integrated by Teilhard into the doctrine of the Eucharist. But what precisely does the synthesis of these two themes achieve by way of mutually illuminating them? The theme of activity and passivity obviously gives to the doctrine of the Eucharist one means at least of extending the notion of eucharistic consecration cosmically. By showing what the bread and wine can symbolize for man, Teilhard is able to indicate that the eucharistic action encompasses the whole of life.

However, it is the enrichment of the theme of activity and passivity by the doctrine of the Eucharist which is most illuminating. Our activity and our suffering are not sufficient of and by themselves to build up the Body of Christ. They need to be transformed. Our activity and suffering are preparatory to this transformation, but the action of Christ is necessary for the actual transformation to take place. We offer all that we are and do and suffer, but this offering can only be consecrated by Christ. Only in this way can communion be achieved. Teilhard's spirituality, like his thought in general, hinges upon a subtle understanding of the dialectical relationship between nature and grace. He does not confuse the orders together but, rather, relates them inseparably together. If we offer nothing, nothing can be transformed, but, what is just as important, no matter how great the plenitude we offer, it is insufficient for the building up of the Body or the coming of the Kingdom. It must be transformed. The natural plenitude of the world becomes the plenitude of Christ through transformation, and the proper understanding of this transforming transposition of one order into the other must be rooted in an understanding of the eucharistic consecration.

The mystery of the Eucharist unquestionably proves an indispensable key to understanding Teilhard's thought. The Protestant theologian, Ernst Benz, sees the importance of the theme in this way:

For Teilhard de Chardin, the original image of evolution is the transformation of the material part of the elements into the body and blood of Christ through the Mass. The transformation which matter undergoes by proceeding from the first to the highest stage of evolution, the stage of christification, is represented mystically and subsequently executed sacramentally by the Mass. . . .

The transformation of the bread and wine into the body and blood of Christ is the mystery, experienced anew every day, which appears to him as the model of evolution of the entire universe and of the total development of life between Alpha and Omega.... Evolution is identical with the *eucharistisation* of the universe, the transformation of the cosmos into the body of Christ.[21]

The passage from cosmogenesis to Christogenesis involves a fundamentally eucharistic operation—the transformation and transfinalization of the Body of the cosmos into the Body of Christ. However, the traditional understanding of transubstantiation makes it necessary for Teilhard to qualify the relationship between the consecration of the bread and the wine and the consecration of the cosmos. Following the Aristotelian model used to interpret transubstantiation, the substances of the bread and the wine are transformed into the substance of the body and blood of Christ, while only the appearances, the accidents, of bread and wine remain. Such an understanding of the Eucharist makes it necessary to say that one formal principle has simply been replaced by another, the bread and wine ceasing to be what they were. The relation of Christ to the cosmos, on the other hand, can only be understood in terms of a quasi-formal causality through which the immanent forms of the cosmos are not replaced but, rather, are taken up into a higher unity through which they are actually differentiated further and brought to fulfillment. If the Aristotelian model of transubstantiation were used to interpret the relationship of Christ to the cosmos, then one would arrive at a pantheistic understanding of Christ's presence in which the cosmos could only be distinguished from Christ accidentally.

However, instead of beginning with a preëstablished understanding of the Eucharist which has subsequently to be qualified in order to make it a suitable model for interpreting the eucharistization of the cosmos, might it not be possible to work in the reverse order, starting with the quasi-formal relationship of Christ to the cosmos as the model for understanding Christ's presence in the Eucharist? If, as Benz suggests, the bread and wine represent the whole of the material dimension, and more particularly the totality of man's activity and suffering, as Teilhard insists, would it not be more probable that the eucharistic transformation of the bread and wine represents the archetypal model of Christ's transforming presence in the cosmos. Consequently, instead of the bread and wine losing their proper identity and retaining only their accidental properties, they would be further differentiated and brought to fulfillment. In other words, they would be truly transformed but not destroyed. The eucharistic consecration would thus, as Benz notes, resume in a liturgical context the history of matter in successive transformations from brute matter through living matter to hominized matter and finally to Christic matter. Such a view of the Eucharist would not necessitate an "impanationist" interpretation, as if the bread and wine were simply juxtaposed with the presence of Christ, for the bread and wine are truly transformed but without losing their identity.

The sacrament of the Eucharist has traditionally been considered in Catholic theology as the sacrament of unity.[22] It is this emphasis which Teilhard makes his own at the same time that he draws out its implications in such a way that the notion of transubstantiation or eucharistization is given a cosmic extension. The doctrine of the Eucharist in Teilhard underlines with unparalleled clarity his own insistence on the necessity of union through transformation and transformation through union. And if the Eucharist is considered to be the sacrament of unity par excellence, it is because it is also considered to be the sacrament of love par excellence. We have already seen that love is the very energy of unification for Teilhard, and now we should like to show how Teilhard reinterprets the traditional understanding of the vices and virtues in terms of multiplicity and unity.

Purity and Charity: The Virtues of Unity

Man, as the axis of the evolutionary movement, has it within his power to carry that movement ahead in the direction of spirit and synthesis or backwards in the direction of matter and multiplicity. In other words, man in his freedom can associate himself with the dynamic thrust of spirit into the future or with the entropic thrust of matter into the past. As we saw in relation to the doctrine of hell in Teilhard's system, man's freedom is confronted with two alternative options, and these two options spell either supreme life or supreme death, all or nothing, for man. Thus it is again within the context of the problem of the one and the many that

Teilhard seeks to understand both vice and virtue as aspects of man's ascent to unity or his descent into multiplicity.

Inasmuch as we have already investigated the role of love as the energy of unification in evolution, we wish now only to show how Teilhard dealt with love, the virtue of collective unity, in his early writings in conjunction with purity, the virtue of personal unity.

The pure of heart, Teilhard tells us, have associated themselves with the dynamic movement of spirit towards unity and simplicity, for it is the specific function of purity to unify the person:

Whereas the sinner, who surrenders himself up to his passions, fragments and dissociates his spirit, the saint, by an inverse process, escapes from the complexity of his affections, by which complexity the memory and trace of their original plurality are kept alive in us. By this very fact, *he becomes gradually less material.* For the saint, everything is God and God is everything. And at the same time Jesus is for him both God and everything. . . . The *specific function of purity* (its formal effect, as the Scholastics would say) therefore *is to unify the interior powers of the soul* in an act of single-minded passion, which is both extraordinarily rich and intense. And finally, the pure soul, transcending the fragmenting and disorganizing attraction of things, immerses his own unity (i.e. develops his spirituality) in the flames of the divine simplicity.[23]

Teilhard almost seems here to echo St. Augustine's line in *The Confessions:* "For by continence we are collected and bound up into unity within ourselves, whereas we had been scattered abroad in multiplicity."[24] For Teilhard, as for Kierkegaard, "purity of heart is to will one thing,"[25] and in this act of willing but one thing, "the one thing necessary,"[26] the person becomes unified, receptive to the action of God in and through him. Through purity, the Christian grows in the divine milieu[27] and his attitude becomes essentially that of Mary, the Mother of Christ: *"Fiat mihi secundum verbum tuum"* (Luke 1, 38).

If purity unifies the multiplicity of our affections, desires, and motivations, charity serves to unify persons with one another.

What purity accomplishes for the interior life of the individual, charity realizes within the collectivity of souls. . . . We will be judged on charity, condemned or justified in terms of it. Why this insistence on charity? If it were merely a matter of philanthropic interest, of the amelioration of our earthly suffering, of terrestrial well-being, how would we explain the gravity evident in the tone, promises, and threats of our Savior?

Once again, we are brought face to face with a great mystery veiled by the modest appearance of Christian doctrine. Does not this mystery consist simply in the mystery of spirit whose task it is to build anew on the ruins of multiplicity? No, Christian brotherhood is not designed simply to repair the damages wrought by egoism and soothe the wounds inflicted by human maliciousness. It is something more than a balm poured by the Good Samaritan on the wounds of society. There is an organic and "cosmic" *opus operatum* which charity effects. Charity, by drawing souls together in love, makes them fruitful for a higher nature which is to be born of their union. It ensures their coherence. Little by little, it serves to dissolve their multiplicity. In short, *it spiritualizes the world.*[28]

Having seen how Teilhard understands purity and charity in relation to the unification of the person and the collectivity,[29] we may now turn our attention to Teilhard's treatment of sensuality and pride as the opposed vices to these virtues, vices which lead not to unity but to multiplicity.

Teilhard begins his discussion of this aspect of the question with one of his few explicit characterizations of the nature of sin:

Sin, in terms of the freedom which commits it, is first of all nothing more than a misguided and particularized attempt to achieve synthesis, the uniquely desirable goal of being. The various concupiscences seduce us by the *lure of unity.*[30]

Teilhard here insists on the traditional doctrine that evil is never chosen for evil's sake but only under the appearance of good. What is more important, Teilhard also defines the nature of sin in a way which not only coheres perfectly with his own system, but which also recalls an ancient traditional understanding of sin. As Henri de Lubac aptly observes:

Following many other spiritual authors, Teilhard underlined sin's disintegrating effects; and from the perspective of his own evolutionary world view, he rediscovered an important dogmatic tradition, which had been allowed to lie dormant: *Ubi peccata, ibi multitudo.*[31]

For Teilhard, sin is a "positive act of disunion,"[32] the choice by man of the descending route of evolution leading back to matter and multiplicity; a choice, however, which is made in the erroneous conviction that this road leads to union, that by following this road, one will achieve fulfillment. Sin is, in short, an abortive attempt to belong which leads in the end only to isolation.

The principal modalities of sin for Teilhard are sensuality and pride:

The first and most uncomplicated form of sin is the concupiscence of the flesh which holds out beneath us the tempting image of a facile return to total matter. Making clever use of a false perspective which creates the illusion that somewhere infinitely far behind us there exists *a point of universal confluence*, the concupiscence of the flesh persuades us that all things are to be joined together through matter, in the depths of the undifferentiated and the unconscious. "The direction of spirit is a dead-end street, it whispers in our ear. The concentration of the soul only serves to widen the fissures which bring suffering upon the world. Let us put a halt to the upward ascent." Whoever listens to the Sirens' song is lost forever. He is only going to swell the number of those who claim to be able to conquer multiplicity by immersing themselves in it and wedding themselves to it forever.

Attempting to achieve unification in a more refined and exactly contrary way, the man inebriated by the concupiscence of the spirit believes that he can transcend the painful fragmentation of beings by reducing them all to his own unity. The proud man makes himself the center of the universe by bestowing an absolute value on that other perspective which causes us to see the world as radiating from ourselves and as it were kneeling down in adoration before us. Everything has to group itself and docilely seek its natural order around such a man.

Whether he is sensual or proud, the sinner hopes to achieve happiness, each in his own way, by suppressing plurality. Unfortunately, he only succeeds in either *reëstablishing multiplicity* in a form long ago transcended by the movement of evolution or in causing it to reappear in a new form, proper to spirit and hence more dangerous and destructive than it ever was.[33]

There undoubtedly exists a connection between Teilhard's treatment of the virtues and vices in terms of unity and multiplicity and his theory of creative union. This is reasonably clear from the fact that it occurs in its most developed and extended form in two essays devoted to the elaboration of that theory.[34] Since this is the case, the virtues of purity and charity must be considered properly creative virtues, since they are essentially unitive virtues, and for Teilhard to unite is to create.

By way of conclusion, we may just note the relationship between this theme and several other themes which we have already considered. Since sensuality and pride are considered by Teilhard as modalities of sin in general, this theme serves to shed further light on Teilhard's understanding of original sin in man. Beginning with a general notion of original sin (or simply sin) as the flight into multiplicity, Teilhard here clarifies the modalities of this flight in terms of two false understandings of matter (sensuality) and spirit (pride). For Teilhard, matter and spirit represent two directional vectors, the one descending into multiplicity in the past, the other ascending into unity in the future. Thus purity and charity constitute the modalities of the world's spiritualization through man, while sensuality and pride constitute the modalities of the world's materialization through man.

Through purity and charity, spirit, the principle of unification, continually gains the ascendency over matter, the principle of dissociation. And the more spirit dominates, the better able it is to unify matter and thus associate matter in its own inner dynamics towards further synthesis. Matter becomes more supple, more responsive to the unitive exigencies of spirit, in this way losing to some extent its own inherent tendency to fragmentation. Through purity and charity, man is able to make matter a cooperator in the growth of his own spiritual life and the spiritual life of mankind as a whole. In other words, through purity and charity, spirit grows and concomitantly matter becomes increasingly caught up in the forwards thrust of spirit, that is, matter becomes spirit without, however, ceasing to be matter. Or perhaps we could even go so far as to say that since the properties of matter, particularly its disintegrating properties, are reversed, it does cease to be matter, *as we are familiar with it*. This ultimate spiritualization of matter, however, would be reserved to the resurrection of the body.

Now, if we turn the preceding chain of arguments upside down, we see that sensuality and pride cause a materialization of spirit. Through sin, man is caught up in the negativity of existence and hence in the dynamics of matter as a vector towards multiplicity. However, to move in the direction of multiplicity is to move in the direction of decreasing spiritualization or increasing materialization. As multiplicity increases, spirit decreases until we reach a point of maximal materialization. Spirit then becomes matter without, however, ceasing to be spirit. Or to employ once again the terms used above, we may say that since the properties of spirit, particularly its unitive properties, are reversed, it ceases to be spirit, *as we are familiar with it*. And in line with this, the ultimate materialization of spirit coincides with hell, a state, as Teilhard insists, completely beyond our ken.

Here the role of freedom in Teilhard's system emerges into full view. Man is situated on a road which extends backwards into the past and forwards into the future. He has to make a choice between these two directions, for in his freedom lies the power to move matter forwards to total spiritualization or spirit backwards to total materialization. Man has it in his power either to invert the properties of matter or to invert the properties of spirit. Man can through his freedom either unify matter, the principle of dissociation, or fragment spirit, the principle of unification. The key to evolution's direction, then, is man's freedom. But man is incapable of opting once and for all for either one of these directions, at least in history. His freedom is engaged in a struggle, the struggle between life and entropy. His freedom is at one and the same time drawn upwards by the current of life and downwards by the current of entropy. Through purity and charity man associates himself with the growth of life, the movement of creativity; through sensuality and egoism, he associates himself with the current of entropy, the movement of destructivity. Heaven or hell, plenitude or emptiness, supreme life or supreme death, all or nothing. These are the alternatives. Would it be too much to say that Teilhard has translated into an evolutionary, contemporary framework St. Augustine's *City of God*?

Pantheism

In our discussion of love and the formula *"l'union différencie,"* as well as in our discussion of the relationship between the natural and the supernatural, we have already tried to show that Teilhard can hardly be considered to be a pantheist. In this chapter devoted to Teilhard's spirituality, we should like to explore Teilhard's own explicit treatment of the problem of pantheism and attempt to determine the precise sense in which he was willing to term himself a "pantheist."

In his autobiographical essay "Le Cœur de la matière," Teilhard himself tells us of his early fascination with pantheism.

In fact, without realizing it, I found that I had, in the course of my awakening to the cosmic life, reached a dead-end from which I could find no exit without the intervention of some new force or some new light. A dead-end. Or rather, a subtle inclination towards an inferior form (the banal and facile form) of the pantheistic spirit: the pantheism of effusion and dissolution. For if the initial call which I had heard indeed came from matter, why (someone within myself whispered to me), why not seek out the essence, the "heart" of matter, in the very direction where all things are "ultra-materialized"; that is in precisely the direction of those most *simple* and enveloping realities which had been but recently revealed to me by the science of energy and of "ether" (as we used to say at that time). In other words, in order to escape from the remorseless fragility of multiplicity, why not plunge down deeper still, beneath multiplicity as it were?[35]

Since this text from 1950 refers specifically to Teilhard's early period and attempts to describe what must be considered a temptation rather than an actual commitment on Teilhard's part, we may now return to the early essays to see how Teilhard dealt with the problem of pantheism at that time and how this early point of view developed subsequently.

Writing to his cousin in July of 1915, Teilhard is seen to have already begun to work out a distinction between two forms of pantheism: "Looked at in one way, nature is a drug, lulling us to sleep in the cradle of nirvana and all the ancient pantheism; in a more real way, she is a penetrating invitation to the slow, patient, and unseen efforts by which the individual, himself borne along by a whole past, humbly prepares a world he will never himself see."[36] The pantheism which Teilhard rejects is what he terms "pagan pantheism."[37] Later, he will oppose his own personalistic pantheism, "the Christian solution" as opposed to "the pantheist solution,"[38] to this pagan pantheism in such a way as to incorporate its deepest aspirations at the same time that he reverses its directionality.[39] Thus, by spiritualizing and personalizing the aspirations of pantheism he is able to transform it in much the same way that he is able to transform matter by reversing its directionality. And the key to transformation in both cases is the same: the person. For the person through his freedom is able to endow matter with either a descending or ascending directionality, just as he is able to endow that "*fundamental,* stubborn, incurable *desire for total union*"[40] (the cosmic sense[41]) with either an ascending (personalizing) or descending (depersonalizing) directionality.

Because "union presupposes, to the limit of its perfection, *duality within unification,*"[42] no form of pantheism can be acceptable which fuses together persons in an undifferentiated state or which destroys the distinction between God and the world. Teilhard's understanding of Christ's quasi-formal relationship to the creation allows for the most intimate kind of immanent presence of God to his creation at the same time that it safeguards God's transcendence.[43] Furthermore, such a form of presence also allows for the most intimate kind of communion between the transcendent personal Center and the finite personal centers at the same time that it posits the fulfilling differentiation or personalization of the latter.[44] Teilhard is thus able to arrive at a Christian form of pantheism in which God and the creatures are brought into communion at the same time that persons and the created order as a whole are maximally differentiated.

In 1923, the reflections of the First World War are condensed and resumed in an essay devoted to the relationship between Christianity and pantheism. Teilhard remarks at the opening of this essay that

usually, the confrontation between these two currents (when made by a Christian) involves an attempt to underscore the opposition between them and to widen even further the gulf which separates them.

My own method of procedure in this essay will be exactly the opposite. I propose to compare pantheism and Christianity here with a view to disengaging what one could call the "Christian soul of pantheism" or the "pantheistic face of Christianity."[45]

We have already seen that during the First World War Teilhard was attempting only to redirect pantheism, and that he saw in Christianity the fulfillment of his own pantheistic aspirations and those of the contemporary world. Teilhard may also have in mind here the article on "Pantheism" written by his friend Auguste Valensin during the summer of 1919, an article with which Teilhard was not at all happy.[46]

In order to bring about the christianization of pantheism, Teilhard in this essay focuses on precisely those elements which we have seen bulk so large in the First World War essays: the incarnation and the mystical Body of Christ understood both physically (or organically) and personalistically.[47] Christianity for Teilhard is indeed a pantheistic religion in the sense that it is also "preoccupied with the totality,"[48] but a world of personalism separates it from pagan forms of pantheism. These two forms of pantheism may in fact share the same fundamental concerns and aspirations, but they are moving in opposite directions towards the fulfillment of their goals.

In 1932 these two directions are more specifically identified. probably as a result of Teilhard's years in China. The opposition between pagan and Christian pantheism is now replaced with the opposition between the way of the East and the way of the West, two opposed but closely connected responses to the problem of the one and the many in the context of spirituality.

There can be no conquering religion without mysticism. And there can be no truly profound mysticism apart from some faith in the unification of the world. The one and the many. Whence the fragmentation of being and how is the return to union to be accomplished? The increasingly distinct perception of this problem, and the gradual approach to its solution, very probably provide us with the means of measuring the stages, not all of which have yet been traversed, of anthropogenesis.[49]

Teilhard then tells us that the purpose of the present essay is "to show how, in continuity with (and at the same time in opposition to) the ancient forms of mysticism (especially the Oriental ones), contemporary humanity, given birth by Western science, is in process, despite the appearance of skeptical positivism, of beginning once again, by a new route, the constant stubborn effort which seems to have driven life in the direction of some fulfilling unity."[50] What is emerging, then, according to Teilhard, is a new form of mysticism seeking to respond to the age-old problem of the one and the many.

Although Christianity itself has been contaminated, in Teilhard's mind, by Oriental mystical influences, the new mysticism of the West will be born from the synthesis of Christian mysticism and the Western evolutionary world view.[51] Once again we see that Christianity must be reformed or developed if it is to be viable as

the religion of the future. As Teilhard remarks in one of his earliest
apologetic essays:

There is, in *The Exercises* of St. Ignatius, a chapter entitled "*ad sentien-
dum cum Matre Ecclesia.*" —However, let us not forget that the
Church, in order to be a true mother, must know how to reciprocate
and "*sentire cum hominibus.*" [52]

The Church must be continually open to both the insights and
needs of the world which she is called to serve if she hopes to be
relevant. This is true in the area of spirituality as well as in the
area of dogma, since the two mutually penetrate one another.

The new mysticism of the West, based as it is on "the idea of a
unity of convergence" [53] is "the first mysticism whose subject is
explicitly the world rather than the human monad." [54] Such a mysticism does not destroy the many but, rather, unifies and differentiates
it at the same time. While the Hindu saint "seeks to isolate himself
from multiplicity," the Christian "works to concentrate and purify
it." [55] "Just like the way of the East, the way of the West leads to
ecstasy through asceticism. Only 'the spirit' is changed—nothing
more." [56] But this change of spirit implies a tremendous change in
one's attitude to the world and to the necessity and role of human
activity in achieving final ecstasy through the completion of the
whole cosmos. For, the completion of the world through man's
activity becomes for Teilhard the "necessary but insufficient condition" for the parousia's occurrence, [57] the moment of supreme
ecstasy for the Christian.

In the years following the writing of "La Route de l'Ouest,"
Teilhard will simply develop the main lines of this opposition between these two ways, "the spirit of fusion" and "the spirit of
amorization," [58] "the spirit of identification" and "the spirit of
unification," [59] "the way of simplification" and "the way of synthesis." [60] The role of the person lies at the heart of the opposition
between these forms of pantheism, for "the only definition of
genuine pantheism" can be "union through personalization and
personalization through union." [61] And because the person stands at
the center of Teilhard's pantheism, so also does love:

Obviously, such a "pan-Christic" monism has quite peculiar characteristics. Because, from the Christian point of view, the universe is
definitively unified only by means of personal relationships, that is

through the influence of love, the unification of beings in God could not be conceived of as taking place through fusion . . . but rather it must be conceived of as taking place through "differentiating" synthesis.[62]

The choice between these forms of pantheism lies with man. Either he must seek "a unity at the base" of the cone of evolution "through dissolution," or "a unity at the summit" of the cone "through ultra-personalization."[63] Either he must follow the route of matter back towards the past of unconsciousness, or he must follow the route of spirit ahead towards the future of full consciousness. The doctrine of the void or the doctrine of the pleroma. For Teilhard himself, the option to be made was perfectly clear. "I am a pilgrim of the future," he tells his cousin, "on my way back from a journey made entirely in the past."[64] Having investigated the structure of the past, Teilhard sets his face resolutely towards the future of mankind: *"The past has revealed to me how the future is built* and preoccupation with the future tends to sweep everything else aside."[65] It is into the future, the future of synthesis and personalization, that man must move.

Summary

Teilhard looks forward in hope to the time when God will be all in all (1 Corinthians 15, 28).[66] Not that God will have then become the all or that the all will have then become God, for at the most intimate stage of union the differences remain and are in fact heightened. In the end, the many will have become one in the One without, however, ceasing to be many. From pure multiplicity to the unification of the many in God through love, the whole movement of evolution is seen to be one long, sustained effort to resolve the problem of the one and the many inherent in being. And if this problem has given structure to an immense, magnificent system of thought reflected upon for over half a century, it is also now seen to have structured a spirituality intensely lived over the same period of time. Teilhard's spirituality flows spontaneously from his system of thought, both of which may be summed up in his own formula: "In all things, to promote and undergo the organic unity of the world."[67]

Teilhard's spirituality is a spirituality lived within the ambiance of the divine milieu, the Body of Christ in its mystical and cosmic dimensions, and activated by a desire to bring the Body of Christ to completion in the pleroma. Through both activity and passivity man serves this work of unification, which finds its most expressive symbolization and realization in the eucharistic celebration which continually reënacts our passage from the Egypt of multiplicity to the Promised Land of unity. Rooted in a pantheism of unifying omnipresence in the divine milieu, Teilhardian spirituality is consummated in the pantheism of union in the pleroma when God will be all in all.

Et tunc erit finis.

Like an immense tide, Being will dominate the trembling of the beings. In the womb of a new placid ocean, in which each drop of water will, however, be conscious of still being itself, the extraordinary adventure of the world will come to an end. The dream of every mystic, the eternal hope of the pantheist, will have found their full and legitimate satisfaction. *"Erit in omnibus omnia Deus."*[68]

And God will be all in all.

Concluding Summary

The purpose of this concluding summary is not to rehearse all the points made in the course of the foregoing discussion but, rather, to draw together the main lines of our argument.

At the beginning of Chapter I, we noted that, according to Teilhard, "science, philosophy, and religion alike have all been basically concerned with the resolution of but one single problem: that of the relationship between multiplicity and unity." Whether or not general agreement could be secured as to the accuracy of Teilhard's description of the fundamental problematic of these areas is beside the point. What we have tried to show is that such a problematic does indeed structure Teilhard's own reflection in these areas. It may further be suggested that Teilhard sees in this common problematic a means of unifying science, philosophy, and religion in such a way that they would all converge upon one another without, however, losing their own proper distinctiveness and limitations. Each of these areas makes its own indispensable contribution to the description and resolution of this problem, and hence these three areas together are necessary for a full understanding of the problem. Their combined efforts are, moreover, essential for an adequate approach to the solution of this problem in both thought and action. Teilhard was a man driven by the passion for unity, and his efforts to synthesize the various spheres of human reflection and activity constitute one of the most important aspects of his overall attempt to resolve the problem of the one and the many, to create unity where pluralistic fragmentation appears to reign supreme.

We also noted at the beginning of Chapter I that for Teilhard the problem of the one and the many is fundamentally a threefold problem. When man reflects upon the relationship between spirit and matter, or between the person and the community, or between God and his creatures, in each instance, according to Teilhard, he is brought face to face with the problem of the one and the many. And in each case Teilhard tries to understand these relationships in such a way that the multiple can be unified without being destroyed. His thought is not monistic but, rather, dipolar or dialectical in character, seeking always to safeguard diversity within unity. The essence of Teilhard's approach is capsulized in his own formula "union differentiates." This is Teilhard's law, if one may so state the matter, and at no point in his system does he violate it in the interests of a simplistic solution which would sacrifice authentic union in favor of an undifferentiated identity.

Given Teilhard's overarching concern with the problem of the one and the many and his determination to avoid the simple elimination of the many, we have taken the notion of union to be the basic category of Teilhard's system. The whole purpose and meaning of the evolutionary process is to achieve increasingly higher forms of union. And the ultimate goal of this process is the union of all things in God, the pleroma or Omega Point of evolutionary history. Thus for Teilhard the evolutionary process begins from a state of extreme multiplicity, the multiplicity of a primitive *Weltstoff*, proceeds through various stages of union (pre-life, life, man), and culminates in the union of all things in God.

When we consider the beginning of the evolutionary process in relation to its end, it is only too obvious that through the intervening stages something new has come into being through union; novelty has appeared. The end is not the beginning. The evolutionary process does not consist in a return to its beginning. Something new has been created between the beginning and the end. Union is thus seen to be properly creative in the sense that novelty emerges. The dynamism of the evolutionary process may therefore be characterized as a creative union. Evolution or creation, depending on one's point of view, proceeds through union. Creation cannot be reduced to a single or even a series of divine acts in the remote past but must, rather, be considered as a continuous process of unification and synthesis. "Creation takes place through a process of unification; and true union comes about only through creation. These two propositions are correlative."[1] Union appears to be the modality of God's creative activity.[2] The theory of creative union may be said to constitute an attempt to grasp the dynamics of creation understood as a continuous evolutionary process rather than as an act in the past.

If the theory of creative union is meant to be employed as a hermeneutical tool for the interpretation of the dynamics of an evolutionary creation, can it effectively deal with the problem of the one and the many as a threefold problem of the relationship of matter and spirit, person and community, creatures and God? In other words, how does the theory of creative union delineate the structure of the creative movement in terms of these three relationships?

Picturing the initial state of creation under the form of an extreme multiplicity, a multiplicity of *Weltstoff* which is neither matter nor spirit alone but rather matter-spirit, Teilhard argues that the complexification of the material pole of this primitive *Weltstoff* is accompanied by a growth of the pole of spirit. The difficult question of causality is deliberately left aside here because Teilhard maintains that he is proceeding descriptively or phenomenologically and is not concerned with philosophical issues. In point of fact, the causal question is not particularly relevant to Teilhard's deepest intention, inasmuch as he is trying to discern a pattern of development, to discover purpose and meaning in the phenomenological evidence. The process of complexification seems indeed to Teilhard to be a directed one, and its directionality can be expressed in the term "spiritualization." The process of unification is directed towards higher forms of spirit and consciousness.

This movement which characterizes the stages of pre-life and life attains to a critical threshold which is successfully crossed with the step of reflection, the appearance of man. Something truly new has now appeared which is continuous with the past stages of evolution, but which at the same time is discontinuous with them in that it marks a transformation, a hominization, of matter-spirit. If the problematic of the stages of pre-life and life can accurately be characterized in terms of the relationship between spirit (the one) and matter (the many), the problematic of the stage of hominized life must be characterized rather in terms of the person (the many) and the community (the one), although the matter-spirit relationship will still continue to play a subsidiary role within this problematic and also serve to provide helpful analogues for the understanding of the person-community relationship.

The law of complexity-consciousness which provides what Teilhard terms an "Ariadne's thread"[3] through the maze of pre-life and life continues to be relevant at the stage of hominization, since the complexification of the material matrix of man's communal relationships plays an important part in the growth of human consciousness. However, here again it can be allowed to play but a subsidiary role in the resolution of the problem of the one and the many in its hominized form. For the problem at this stage of evolution is how to unify persons together in community, how to achieve an authentic union of persons which will be properly creative of genuine personhood. The complexification of the material matrix of man's life is insufficient, if nonetheless indispensable, for this.

A new unifying factor enters into the picture at this point, although it has not been absent at the pre-hominized stages of evolution. That factor is love. Only love can achieve the unification of human persons in community at the same time that it safeguards and indeed leads to authentic personhood. However, when Teilhard comes to inspect the forms of love-energy immediately available to man in the noosphere for the accomplishing of this task, he finds them all to be both limited and ambiguous. While they do indeed unite, they only unite limited segments of the noosphere at the same time that they tend to create new antagonisms and divisions. What is clearly needed is a form of love capable of embracing the whole noosphere. It is the quest for this universal form of love which leads Teilhard to the Church as a phenomenologically observable constituent of the noosphere which claims, however, to be grounded in a reality and power which transcends the purely immanent factors in the evolutionary movement.

The Church serves to prove for Teilhard that the universal form of love necessary for the completion of evolution is both psychologically possible and historically realizable for man. Man is thus given a meaningful future by the Church, for he is allowed through the example of the Church to see that the unity which he desires and knows to be necessary is not merely an ideal but a realizable possibility. The Church also serves to point beyond itself to Christ as the transcendent personal Center capable of activating within the whole of humanity the kind of love needed for final unity. It also can be shown, Teilhard believes, that the Christ experienced in faith by the Christian community correlates in a striking way with the Omega Point whose existence has to be postulated by reason on the basis of the exigencies of the evolutionary movement.

This whole line of argument, beginning with the hominized form of the problem of the one and the many and culminating in the correlation of the cosmic Christ with Omega Point, may properly be characterized as the apologetical side of Teilhard's system, but it is intimately connected with the theme of union which in the context of hominization increasingly depends upon the activation of a universal form of love. What we are here calling the "apologetical side" of Teilhard's system also corresponds for the most part with the structure of *The Phenomenon of Man*, but seen in the light of the notion of creative union. Although Teilhard does not employ this expression in that work, he does invite us to read it from such a point of view when he says that "fuller being consists in closer union: such is the kernel and conclusion of this book."[4]

In addition to and in strict continuity with this apologetical line of argument addressed to the unbeliever, we also find a line of properly theological argument addressed to the believer. Teilhard's theological reflection is not systematic in form but, rather, focuses on the areas of ecclesiology and christology as these relate to the problem of creation as a continuous process of unification. Teilhard's ecclesiological reflection centers on the notion of the Church as the Body of Christ. This specifically theological notion dovetails remarkably well with Teilhard's understanding of the multiplicity of mankind as a new matter which has to be unified into a new Body by a new Spirit. However, instead of developing the traditional doctrine of the Holy Spirit as the Soul of the Body of Christ as we might have expected at this point, Teilhard identifies this Soul with the cosmic Christ who thus becomes the quasi-formal cause of the unity of the Church.

However, if Christ is to be understood as the unifying quasi-formal cause of the Church, his unifying role is not to be restricted to the Church. For in addition to his mystical Body which is the Church, Christ also animates a cosmic Body which is the world. It is not in all respects clear just how Teilhard understands the relationship between these two Bodies, but it is at least clear that he does not simply intend to broaden the concept of the Church in such a way that it merges imperceptibly with the world. The Church holds a privileged position in Teilhard's view as the axis of evolution which bears witness to what the world can become in the future through the unifying power of a universal love.

Perhaps the simplest way to understand the relationship between the two Bodies is to think of the Church as the mediational focus of Christ's unifying activity in the world—through the Church Christ acts to unify the world also. Whatever the ambiguities and uncertainties attaching to the relationship between the Church (the mystical Body) and the world (the cosmic Body) in history, these ambiguities and uncertainties will be dissolved in the final unity of all things in God (the pleroma) in which any distinction between the two Bodies will cease to exist. It is also within the context of the pleroma that the problem of the one and the many as a problem concerning the relationship between God and the creatures will be resolved, although it is already in process of resolution within history through the unifying activity of Christ in the Church and in the world.

Both the apologetical and theological sides of Teilhard's reflection are permeated by the problem of the one and the many and the category of union. Teilhard finds in the resolution of the problem of the one and the many as a problem of the relationship between God and the creatures the resolution of the problem of the one and the many as a problem of the relationship between the person and the community. In both cases the resolution of the problematic comes about through Christ, who activates the kind of universal love needed for the organic unity of mankind and who is also present as the vivifying Center, indeed Soul, of this organic unity. The problem of the relationship between the person and the community is thus seen to be intrinsically linked with the problem of man's relationship to God. The creative union of mankind can ultimately take place only in Christ. We may conclude that the theory of creative union constitutes a fundamentally theological approach to the resolution of the problem of the one and the many.

It has often enough been contended that Teilhard's view of evolutionary process is unduly and unwarrantedly optimistic, and our summary of Teilhard's position up to this point would seem to lend credence to such a view. Do we in fact find in Teilhard simply an evolutionary process of unification moving blissfully towards its completion in God? Is it not rather the case that it is the problem

6

of evil as Teilhard understands it which really makes the problem of the one and the many a genuinely acute one for him. Matter is not simply a fertile matrix for the growth of spirit; in fact, it can be characterized as a directional vector towards multiplicity which spells death for spirit. The person does not enter easily and readily into the interests and purposes of the communal growth of mankind; in fact, the creature represents still another directional vector towards the non-being which is multiplicity. In short, the many resist unity, and hence union can be achieved only by overcoming this resistance through struggle.

The problem of evil is neither sleighted nor under-estimated by Teilhard, but he is compelled to reinterpret it in the light of his understanding of creation as a continuous process. If we may describe Teilhard's understanding of evil fundamentally as a flight from union, then evil is concomitant with creation itself. Matter flees from spirit, the person flees from community, the creature flees from God. What is the origin of this inclination towards flight into multiplicity and non-being? It can hardly originate with man in an evolutionary world view. However, it is hardly more satisfactory to say, as Teilhard does, that evil is simply a by-product of the evolutionary process, a statistical necessity. At any rate, Teilhard's real contribution to an understanding of the problem of evil is not in terms of origins but, rather, in terms of the phenomenological description of evil as the flight into multiplicity, as the attempt to make the world of creation irreducibly pluralistic.

The tendency of matter towards disintegration finds expression in Teilhard's thought in the concept of entropy, whereas the tendency of the person towards the disintegration of community through pride and sensuality finds expression in the concept of original sin. However, for Teilhard the term "original sin," like the term "creation," can only be understood in a rather limited sense as an act in the remote past. Which is only to say that his principal concern is not with the traditional notion of original sin as an act of mankind's first parents at all but, rather, with the problem of evil in general which he illegitimately tries to treat under the single rubric of original sin. Teilhard can only logically say that evil is modalized in different ways at different stages of the evolutionary movement, that physical and moral evil are different modalities of evil in general, and that they are causally unconnected even if physical evil

is considerably aggravated by the appearance of a properly hominized form of evil.

Because for Teilhard the evolutionary process involves a growth
in consciousness, it also necessarily involves a growth in the possibilities for evil, and these possibilities are frequently enough actual-
ized through sin. However, the disintegrative force of sin is not
allowed to develop unchecked inasmuch as Teilhard thinks of the
redemptive activity of God as also being coextensive with his
total creative activity. In fact, it may be said that the divine redemptive activity is to be considered a modality of the divine
creative activity, and that it expresses the necessity of God's entering into struggle with the forces of disintegration in order to create
by unifying. Both God's creative and redemptive activity are thus
understood in terms of the notion of unification, just as evil is
understood in terms of fragmentation and disintegration. The theory
of creative union is also a theory of redemptive union. The problem
of evil and the doctrine of redemption are understood strictly in
relation to the problem of the one and the many as a problem
of how to unify the many in the face of the disruptive force of
evil.

The Christian's participation in this struggle for unity involves a
spirituality of creative and redemptive union which seeks "in all
things, to promote and undergo the organic unity of the world."[5]
It is thus essentially a spirituality of both activity and passivity
lived within the unifying ambiance of the divine milieu or Body of
Christ. It is a spirituality centered on the Eucharist, the sacrament
of both union and creative transformation. It is a spirituality
focused on the cultivation of the virtues of purity and love, virtues
whose function it is to unify the person and the community respectively. And even in his treatment of the virtues, we see that
Teilhard is seeking once again to resolve the problem of the one
and the many as it is caught up in the problem of evil, for purity
and love are seen to be engaged in a struggle with sensuality and
pride, vices which fragment and scatter the person and the community into multiplicity.

If Teilhardian spirituality is ecclesiological, sacramental, and
ethical in its orientation, it is also mystical in its aspirations. It seeks
not only to discover the divine presence immanent in the world, but
also to be open to the unifying influence of that presence in oneself

and in the larger community of creation. Teilhardian spirituality is a mysticism of union, creative and personalizing union, whose goal is nothing less than the union of all things in God.

Teilhard's system of thought flows easily and naturally into a spirituality. And both aspects of his work are dominated by the problem of the one and the many and the concern to resolve that problem through creative union. As we noted at the beginning of Chapter I, the unification of the multiple in synthetic thought can only be a preliminary step towards the unification of the multiple in synthetic action. We hope to have demonstrated that Teilhard has accomplished an impressive synthesis of both these areas.

Having thus summarized the main line of our argument, we wish only to underline what we consider to be the principal result of our inquiry. We set out initially neither to defend nor to criticize Teilhard but, rather, to achieve a sympathetic understanding of his world view. We feel that the principal result of our inquiry is to have shown that the theory of creative union does in fact provide a fruitful methodological key to achieving such an understanding once Teilhard's central problematic is seen to consist in the resolution of the problem of the one and the many. The only justification we can offer for the validity of our approach is the coherence which it establishes within the totality of Teilhard's system. We may recall that Teilhard himself attempted much the same justification for his own interpretation of the shape of reality.

We have been guided throughout this study by the conviction that any significant thinker deserves to be approached first of all in a spirit of sympathetic openness towards his own deepest intentions and personal point of view. Any perspective carries with it its own intrinsic limitations, but the pinpointing and transcending of these limitations with regard to Teilhard's own world view is a task which must at this point be left to others to carry out.

Notes

List of Abbreviations

Primary Sources

AM: The Appearance of Man (New York, 1966). Translation of Volume II of the *Oeuvres*.

ET: Ecrits du temps de la guerre, 1916–1919 (Paris, 1965). Many of these essays have been translated in either *WTW* or *HU*. Some remain as yet untranslated.

FM: The Future of Man (New York, 1964). Translation of Volume V of the *Oeuvres*.

GP: Genèse d'une pensée, Lettres, 1914–1919 (Paris, 1961).

HU: Hymne de l'univers (Paris, 1961). Eng. trans., *Hymn of the Universe* (New York, 1965).

LT: Letters From a Traveller (New York, 1962). Translation of *LV*.

LV: Lettres de voyage, 1923–1955 (Paris, 1961).

LZ: Lettres à Léontine Zanta (Paris, 1965).

MD: Le Milieu divin, 1926–1927 (Paris, 1957). Eng. trans., *The Divine Milieu* (New York, 1965).

MM: The Making of a Mind (New York, 1965). Translation of *GP*.

Oeuvres: Oeuvres de Pierre Teilhard de Chardin, 9 volumes (Paris, 1955–1965). *PH* and *MD* constitute Volumes I and IV; the other volumes are collections of writings from various periods.

PH: Le Phénomène humain, 1938–1940 (Paris, 1955). Eng. trans., *The Phenomenon of Man* (New York, 1965).

PN: Man's Place in Nature (New York, 1966). Translation of Volume VIII of the *Oeuvres*.

VP: The Vision of the Past (New York, 1967). Translation of Volume III of the *Oeuvres*.

WTW: Writings In Time of War (New York, 1968). This volume includes many, but not all, of the essays contained in *ET*.

Secondary Sources

de Lubac: Henri de Lubac, S.J., *La Pensée religieuse du Père Teilhard de Chardin* (Paris, 1962). Eng. trans., *The Religion of Teilhard de Chardin* (New York, 1967).

Mooney: Christopher Mooney, S.J., *Teilhard de Chardin and the Mystery of Christ* (New York, 1966).

Rideau: Emile Rideau, S.J., *La Pensée du Père Teilhard de Chardin* (Paris, 1965). Eng. trans., *The Thought of Teilhard de Chardin* (New York, 1967).

Smulders: Piet Smulders, S.J., *La Vision de Teilhard de Chardin* (Paris, 1965, 2nd revised edition). Eng. trans., *The Design of Teilhard de Chardin* (Westminster, Md., 1967). The English translation was made from the first French edition of 1964.

de Solages: Bruno de Solages, *Teilhard de Chardin* (n.p., 1967).

Note: An asterisk (*) before an item indicates unpublished material. References to this material cannot always be accurate due to differences in pagination between various copies.

Chapter I

1. "Esquisse d'un univers personnel" (1936), *Oeuvres*, VI, p. 73.

2. *"Comment je vois" (1948), p. 18.

3. *Ibid.*, p. 18.

4. *Ibid.*, pp. 18–19.

5. *Ibid.*, p. 18, n. 27.

6. *Ibid.*, p. 17.

7. *Ibid.*, p. 17, n. 26, where Teilhard explicitly states that "the term 'plura' does not hold good in reference to God in the case of trinitization."

8. On the Trinity as the goal of creation, see Journal entry of October 21, 1922, cited in de Solages, p. 295, n. 89; *"Christianisme et évolution" (1945), p. 7; "Esquisse d'une dialectique de l'esprit," *Oeuvres*, VII, p. 156.

9. "La Lutte contre la multitude" (1917), in *ET*, p. 114; Eng. trans. in *WTW*, p. 95.

10. "L'Union créatrice" (1917), in *ET*, pp. 185–186; Eng. trans. in *WTW*, pp. 163–164.

11. "Mon Univers" (1918), in *ET*, p. 277.

12. "Mon Univers" (1924), *Oeuvres*, IX, p. 74.

13. Claude Tresmontant, *Introduction à la pensée de Teilhard de Chardin* (Paris, 1956), pp. 112–113; Eng. trans. *Pierre Teilhard de Chardin: His Thought* (Baltimore, 1959), p. 91.

14. "Au R. P. Henri de Lubac," *Nova et Vetera*, XXXVII (June–September, 1962), pp. 227–228.

15. Smulders, pp. 90–97; Eng. trans., pp. 77–85.

16. de Lubac, pp. 281–289; Eng. trans. pp. 195–200.

17. *Bergson et Teilhard de Chardin* (Paris, 1963), pp. 607–613.

18. "Schöpfungslehre als 'Physik' und 'Metaphysik' des Einen und Vielen bei Teilhard de Chardin." *Scholastik*, XXXIX (1964), pp. 519–524.

19. *La Pensée théologique de Teilhard de Chardin*, pp. 116–119.

20. Rideau, pp. 330–334; Eng. trans., pp. 152–156.

21. "Les Noms de la matière" (1919), in *ET*, p. 421.

22. "La Paléontologie et l'apparition de l'homme" (1923), *Oeuvres*, II, pp. 80–81; Eng. trans. in *AM*, pp. 56–57. The same thought employing the same image had been expressed earlier in "Science et Christ" (1921), *Oeuvres*, IX, pp. 56–57. Cf. Letter of October 3, 1923, to Léontine Zanta in *LZ*, p. 60.

23. "La Place de l'homme dans l'univers. Réflexions sur la complexité" (1942), *Oeuvres*, III, pp. 323–324; Eng. trans. in *VP*, p. 231. Cf. *"Quelques vues générales sur l'essence du christianisme" (1939), p. 1.

24. Teilhard read Bergson's work during his seminary days at Hastings and it was apparently this book which really opened his eyes to the theory of evolution. Cf. *"Le Coeur de la matière" (1950), p. 8.

25. This formula is used in "Esquisse d'une dialectique de l'esprit" (1946). *Oeuvres*, VII, pp. 152–157; *"Réflexions sur le péché originel" (1947), p. 4; and *"Le Phénomène chrétien" (1950), p. 3.

26. "L'Union créatrice" (1917), in *ET*, p. 179; Eng. trans. in *WTW*, p. 157.

27. *Ibid.*, p. 178; Eng. trans. in *WTW*, p. 156.

28. "Mon Univers" (1924), *Oeuvres*, IX, p. 73.

29. "La Lutte contre la multitude" (1917), in *ET*, p. 114; Eng. trans. in *WTW*, p. 95; *"Comment je vois" (1948), p. 19; "Du Cosmos à la cosmogénèse" (1951), *Oeuvres*, VII, p. 271; *Letter of June 19, 1953, p. 2; *"Le Christique" (1955), p. 1.

30. This expression is already to be found in the Journal entry of January 13, 1919, cited in de Solages, p. 318, n. 41, five years before its appearance in the text of "Mon Univers" which we cited above.

31. "L'Union créatrice" (1917), in *ET*, p. 182; Eng. trans. in *WTW*, pp. 159–160.

32. Cf. Journal entry of August 19, 1917, cited in de Solages, p. 315; Journal entry of May 11, 1920, cited in de Solages, p. 318, n. 41; "Mon Univers" (1924), *Oeuvres*, IX, p. 73; "La Centrologie. Essai d'une dialectique de l'union" (1944), *Oeuvres*, VII, p. 120; *"Comment je vois" (1948), p. 17.

33. *"Comment je vois" (1948), p. 17.

34. Madeleine Barthélemy-Madaule, *Bergson et Teilhard de Chardin*, p. 599, also sees "creative union as the center of the Teilhardian synthesis."

35. Cited in *GP*, p. 50; Eng. trans. in *MM*, p. 37. In a letter to Léontine Zanta, in *LZ*, p. 57, dated August 7, 1923, Teilhard refers to the First World War period as his "intellectual honeymoon."

Chapter II

1. "Mon Univers" (1924), *Oeuvres*, IX, pp. 72–73.

2. *Ibid.*, pp. 73–74.

3. It is important to keep in mind that Teilhard is using the term soul in a sense similar to that of the Scholastics who spoke of a plant (vegetative), animal (sensitive), and human (intelligent) soul. However, Teilhard does not limit the matter/spirit relationship to just living things. In this sense, his

approach is similar to the Scholastic notions of matter and form. For Teilhard as for the Scholastics, there is no such thing as uninformed matter within the limits of our experience. Hence we could say that Teilhard's pure multiplicity resembles the Scholastics' prime matter which is a logical postulate arrived at by abstraction and not an actually existing type of matter.

4. "La Lutte contre la multitude" (1917), in *ET*, p. 115; Eng. trans. in *WTW*, pp. 96–97.

5. "L'Union créatrice" (1917), in *ET*, p. 179; Eng. trans. in *WTW*, p. 157. Cf. "Les Noms de la matière" (1919), in *ET*, p. 420.

6. "Mon Univers" (1918), in *ET*, p. 277.

7. "Le Coeur de la matière" (1950), p. 26.

8. *PH*, p. 57; Eng. trans., pp. 60–61.

9. "L'Avenir de l'homme vu par un paléontologiste" (1941), *Oeuvres*, V., pp. 90–91; Eng. trans. in *FM*, p. 66.

10. *PH*, p. 21; Eng. trans., p. 29.

11. *"Le Coeur de la matière" (1950), p. 24. Cf. "Du Cosmos à la cosmogénèse" (1951), *Oeuvres*, VII, p. 267, where Teilhard defends this manner of speaking against the charge of being implicitly materialistic. Cf. also Rideau, p. 189, n. 21, Eng. trans., p. 392, n. 21, on the etymology of *materia* and its relationship to *mater*.

12. "Esquisse d'un univers personnel" (1936), *Oeuvres*, VI, p. 74.

13. The terms *Weltstoff* and *l'étoffe de l'univers* are used quite regularly from 1936 on. Cf., on this point, Smulders, p. 45, n. 15; Eng. trans., p. 264, n. 15. Claude Cuénot objects that there is not in fact a strict equivalency between *Stoff* in German and *l'étoffe* in French, *Teilhard de Chardin et la pensée catholique* (Paris, 1965), p. 99.

14. "Esquisse d'un univers personnel" (1936), *Oeuvres*, VI, p. 74.

15. "Forma Christi" (1918), in *ET*, pp. 351–352; Eng. trans. in *WTW*, p. 267; "Les Noms de la matière" (1919), in *ET*, p. 426; *"Chute, rédemption, et géocentrie" (1920), p. 4; "Mon Univers" (1924), *Oeuvres*, IX, p. 79. More recently, Karl Rahner, *On the Theology of Death* (New York, 1961), pp. 31–32, has argued in favor of the theological position that the angels are essentially related to the material world, although he denies that they are themselves material.

16. "Les Noms de la matière" (1919), in *ET*, p. 428. Cf. "La Centrologie" (1944), *Oeuvres*, VII, p. 131; "Du Cosmos à la cosmogénèse" (1951), *Oeuvres*, VII, p. 267.

17. "Les Fondements et le fond de l'idée de l'évolution" (1926), *Oeuvres*, III, p. 186; Eng. trans. in *VP*, p. 133.

18. "Mon Univers" (1924), *Oeuvres*, IX, p. 79.

19. "Esquisse d'un univers personnel" (1936), *Oeuvres*, VI, p. 73. Cf. *"Le Coeur de la matière" (1950), p. 9.

20. "La Puissance spirituelle de la matière" (1919), in *ET*, p. 441; Eng. trans. in *HU*, p. 64.

21. Cf. "Les Noms de la matière" (1919), in *ET*, pp. 425–427, 429; *MD*, pp. 125, 127; Eng. trans., pp. 108, 109.

22. Claude Cuénot, "Esprit et matière dans la philosophie de Pierre Teilhard de Chardin" in *Teilhard de Chardin et la pensée catholique* (Paris, 1965), p. 69.

23. *Ibid.*, p. 69.

24. *"L'Evolution de la chasteté" (1934), p. 9. Cf. *MD*, p. 56; Eng. trans., p. 66.
25. "Science et Christ" (1921), *Oeuvres*, IX, p. 55.
26. The expression "tout tient par en-haut" was borrowed by Teilhard from Maurice Blondel and is used by Teilhard in "La Foi qui opère" (1918), in *ET*, p. 322; Eng. trans. in *WTW*, p. 240; "L'Elément universel" (1919), in *ET*, p. 410, n. 8; Eng. trans. in *WTW*, p. 299, n. 9; "Mon Univers" (1924), *Oeuvres*, IX, p. 78; *"Comment je crois" (1934), p. 13; *PH*, p. 37; Eng. trans., p. 43.
27. "Science et Christ" (1921), *Oeuvres*, IX, p. 57.
28. Cf. "Mon Univers" (1918), in *ET*, pp. 276–277; *PH*, pp. 49–50, 186; Eng. trans., pp. 53, 169; *"Le Coeur de la matière" (1950), p. 27; *"Le Christique" (1955), p. 3.
29. "Le Phénomène spirituel" (1937), *Oeuvres*, VI, p. 118.
30. "Science et Christ" (1921), *Oeuvres*, IX, p. 50.
31. *PH*, p. 286; Eng. trans., pp. 257–258.
32. "Esquisse d'un univers personnel" (1936), *Oeuvres*, VI, p. 72. Cf. "L'Energie humaine" (1937), *Oeuvres*. VI, p. 150.
33. *"Le Coeur de la matière" (1950), p. 9.
34. "L'Etoffe de l'univers" (1953), *Oeuvres*, VII, p. 398. Teilhard's "Come and see" is undoubtedly intended to echo John 1, 39.
35. Robert Frost, "The Road Not Taken," *Complete Poems of Robert Frost* (New York, 1960), p. 131.
36. *PH*, p. 62; Eng. trans., pp. 64–65.
37. *Ibid.*, pp. 62–63; Eng. trans., p. 65.
38. *Ibid.*, pp. 63–64; Eng. trans., p. 66.
39. *Ibid.*, p. 301; Eng. trans., p. 270.
40. "L'Analyse de la vie" (1945), *Oeuvres*, VII, p. 139.
41. "Les Mouvements de la vie" (1928), *Oeuvres*, III, p. 209; Eng. trans. in *VP*, p. 149. Cf. "Le Phénomène humain" (1928), *Oeuvres*, IX, pp. 125–126.
42. *"Comment je crois" (1934), p. 10.
43. "La Réflexion de l'énergie" (1952), *Oeuvres*, VII, p. 352.
44. "Le Phénomène humain" (1930), *Oeuvres*, III, p. 237; Eng. trans. in *VP*, p. 169. Cf. "L'Esprit de la terre" (1931), *Oeuvres*, VI, p. 28.
45. "Le Phénomène spirituel" (1937), *Oeuvres*, VI, p. 123.
46. Cf. "Universalisation et Union" (1942), *Oeuvres*, VII, p. 94. "Esquisse d'une dialectique de l'esprit" (1946), *Oeuvres*, VII, p. 150.
47. "La Grande option" (1939), *Oeuvres*, V, p. 69; Eng. trans. in *FM*, pp. 48–49.
48. "Le Phénomène humain" (1930), *Oeuvres*, III, p. 238; Eng. trans. in *VP*, p. 170.
49. "Transformation et prolongements en l'homme du mécanisme de l'évolution" (1951), *Oeuvres*, VII, p. 317; "Un Problème majeur pour l'anthropologie" (1951), *Oeuvres*, VII, p. 330; *"Contingence de l'univers et goût humain de survivre" (1953). p. 1. Rideau, p. 172; Eng. trans., p. 89, notes that the term "negative entropy" or "neg-entropy" is borrowed from Schrödinger. Cf. the interesting remarks of Lucien Morren with regard to the advances made by cybernetics and information theory by way of confirming the notion of neg-entropy: *Teilhard de Chardin et la pensée catholique*, pp. 97–98.
50. "Les Singularités de l'espèce humain" (1954), *Oeuvres*, II, pp. 363–364; Eng. trans. in *AT*, pp. 265–266.

Chapter III

1. *GP* 349–350; Eng. trans. in *MM*, p. 268.
2. "Note pour servir à l'évangélisation des temps nouveaux" (1919), in *ET*, p. 377. Cf. "L'Elément universel" (1919), in *ET*, p. 403; Eng. trans. in *WTW*, p. 292.
3. "Les Noms de la matière" (1919), in *ET*, pp. 426–427. The actual text has *"formes peccati"* rather than *"fomes peccati,"* but this is undoubtedly a misprint.
4. *"Note sur quelques représentations historiques possibles du péché originel" (1922), p. 5. We are following here the dating of this essay suggested by Henri de Lubac, *LZ*, p. 34. De Lubac also gives the details of the difficulties which this essay caused Teilhard vis-à-vis his religious superiors in Rome. De Solages, pp. 42–45, also accepts this date and gives further details on Teilhard's difficulties over the essay.
5. *Ibid.*, p. 6.
6. "Mon Univers" (1924), *Oeuvres*, IX, pp. 108–109 and n. 1. Teilhard associates the notion of involution with that of entropy in "L'Esprit de la terre" (1931), *Oeuvres*, VI, p. 28.
7. *"Réflexions sur le péché originel" (1947), pp. 3–4. In a note to this text Teilhard indicates that by Alexandrian school he really has in mind St. Gregory of Nyssa. He also mentions that this theory had of late been revived and taught at Louvain. De Lubac, p. 167, n. 5, Eng. trans. p. 319, n. 80, informs us that it was Teilhard's close friend Father Pierre Charles, who taught at Louvain, who was championing the position. De Solages, p. 325, n. 61, mentions that this essay was written at his own personal request.
8. *Letter of June 19, 1953, written from New York, pp. 1–2.
9. *Ibid.*, pp. 2–3.
10. de Solages, pp. 326–327.
11. We know that Charles' position influenced the presentation of the Fall in *"Réflexions sur le péché originel" (1947) because de Solages, p. 326, n. 69, tells us that Teilhard had written a manuscript note addressed to him which read "Charles' explanation" when he sent him the essay. There are no other explicit indications of Charles' influence in the other essays dealing with the problem, although such influence could hardly be ruled out on the basis of an *argumentum e silentio*.
12. *"Réflexions sur le péché originel" (1947), p. 4.
13. *Ibid.*, p. 4.
14. *Ibid.*, p. 3.
15. "Mon Univers" (1924), *Oeuvres*, IX, p. 109.
16. *Letter of June 19, 1953, p. 1.
17. *"Quelques représentations historiques possibles du péché originel" (1922), p. 5.
18. See Mooney, pp. 135–143; Georges Crespy, *De la science à la théologie* (Neuchâtel, 1965), pp. 76–83; Rideau, pp. 346–350; Eng. trans. pp. 169–174; Robert Faricy, *Teilhard de Chardin's Theology of the Christian in the World* (New York, 1967), pp. 153–162.
19. To the texts already cited may be added "La Vie cosmique" (1916), in *ET*, pp. 60–61; Eng. trans. in *WTW*, pp. 70–71, and several Journal entries, cited in de Solages, pp. 323–324.

20. "Note sur le Christ-universel" (1920), *Oeuvres*, IX, p. 41.

21. *"Chute, rédemption et géocentrie" (1920), p. 3.

22. *Ibid.*

23. *Ibid.*

24. *"Note sur quelques représentations historiques possibles de péché originel" (1922), pp. 6–7.

25. *"Quelques vues générales sur l'essence du christianisme" (1939), p. 2.

26. *"Le Christ Evoluteur" (1942), p. 9. The Appendix on original sin to this essay from which this text is taken is not included in the published text of the essay in *Cahiers* 5 (Paris, 1965).

27. This formula, with slight modifications in the Latin at times, is used in: *"Notes sur les modes de l'action divine dans l'univers" (1920), p. 10; *"Chute, rédemption et géocentrie" (1920). p. 3; *MD*, p. 89; Eng. trans. p. 86; *PH*, p. 346; Eng. trans., p. 312; *"Le Christ Evoluteur" (1942), p. 9; *"Réflexions sur le péché originel" (1947), p. 5; *"Comment je vois" (1948), p. 20; *Letter of June 19, 1953, p. 1.

28. References may be found in Mooney, p. 244, n. 84.

29. Karl Rahner, *On the Theology of Death*, pp. 40–57.

30. "L'Ame du monde" (1918), in *ET*, p. 231; Eng. trans. in *WTW*, pp. 189–190.

31. *"Note sur quelques représentations historiques possibles du péché originel" (1922), p. 7. Cf. *"Quelques vues générales sur l'essence du christianisme" (1939), p. 1.

32. *"Introduction à la vie chrétienne" (1944), p. 3. Cf. *"Christianisme et évolution" (1945), pp. 7–8.

33. *"Réflexions sur le péché originel" (1947), pp. 6–7. Cf. *"Comment je vois" (1948), p. 19; "Du Cosmos à la cosmogénèse" (1951), *Oeuvres*, VII, p. 271. For further discussion of this theme in Teilhard, see Smulders, pp. 144–150; Eng. trans. pp. 133–139; de Solages, pp. 328–332.

34. Teilhard uses the model of the spiral himself and in roughly the same sense that we are using it here. Cf. "L'Hominisation" (1925), *Oeuvres*, III, p. 92; Eng. trans. in *VP*, p. 63; "Du Pré-humain à l'ultra-humain" (1950), *Oeuvres*, V, p. 381; Eng. trans. in *FM*, p. 293; *"Le Coeur de la matière" (1950), p. 26; "Les Singularités de l'espèce humain" (1954), *Oeuvres*, II, p. 337; Eng. trans. in *AM*, pp. 243–244. The thought, together with an implication of the image, can be clearly seen in the following text: "From circle to circle the world is metamorphosed by undergoing an internal enrichment and transformation. Consequently, each time this happens the world is found to be in a new state, in which the totality of properties formerly present persist in part and are renewed in part." ("Le Phénomène humain" [1928], *Oeuvres*, IX, p. 122). As early as 1916, Teilhard expressed the same point with considerable succinctness: "Everything is made by the transformation of a pre-existing analogue" ("La Maîtrise du monde et le règne de Dieu" [1916], in *ET*, p. 75; Eng. trans. in *WTW*, p. 83).

35. Cf. *PH*, 21; Eng. trans. p. 29; "La Place de l'homme dans l'univers" (1942), *Oeuvres*, III, p. 321; Eng. trans. in *VP*, p. 229; "La Centrologie" (1944), *Oeuvres*, VII, pp. 105, 116, 117, 120, 134; "Esquisse d'une dialectique de l'esprit" (1946), *Oeuvres*, VII, pp. 150, 151; "Vie et planètes" (1946). *Oeuvres*, V, pp. 139, 143, n. 1; Eng. trans. in *FM*, pp. 107, 111, n. 1; "La Formation de la noosphère" (1947), *Oeuvres*, V. pp. 222, 227; Eng. trans. in *FM*. pp. 174, 179; *"Comment je vois" (1948), p. 17; "Les Singularités de

l'espèce humain" (1954), *Oeuvres*, II, p. 338; Eng. trans. in *AM*, pp. 244–245.

36. To the text cited in n. 25 we may add *"Note sur quelques représentations historiques possibles du péché originel" (1922), pp. 7–8.

37. Cf. *"Chute, rédemption et géocentrie" (1920), p. 1; "Que faut-il penser du transformisme" (1930), *Oeuvres*, III, pp. 219–220; Eng. trans. in *VP*, pp. 156–157; *"Christologie et évolution" (1933), p. 3; *"Réflexions sur le péché originel" (1947), p. 6; *"Monogénisme et monophylétisme" (1950), pp. 1–2; Letter of April 28, 1954, cited in T. V. Fleming, S.J., "Two Unpublished Letters of Teilhard," *The Heythrop Journal*, VI (January 1965), pp. 36–37. The more tentative approach to the problem in *PH*, p. 206, n. 1; Eng. trans. p. 186, n. 1, while strictly in keeping with Teilhard's own principles, does not accurately reflect his own convictions as expressed elsewhere and was undoubtedly inserted in the hope of getting the book past the Jesuit censors.

38. Cf. Robert North, S.J., "'Breath in Clay' or Many Adams," *Teilhard and the Creation of the Soul* (Milwaukee, 1967), pp. 35–61. Karl Rahner, who offers a vigorous defense of monogenism in *Theological Investigations*, I (Baltimore, 1961), pp. 229–296, has recently put forward a defense of the polygenistic hypothesis, "Evolution and Original Sin," *The Evolving World and Theology* (New York, 1967), pp. 61–73.

39. What we have been calling Teilhard's own solution to the problem of original sin appears not in fact to have been of his own making. De Solages, p. 327, informs us that Abbé Henri Breuil, Teilhard's colleague and close friend, told de Solages that he had suggested this approach to Teilhard.

Chapter IV

1. "La Lutte contre la multitude" (1917), in *ET*, p. 123; Eng. trans. in *WTW*, p. 105. Cf. "Le Milieu mystique" (1917), in *ET*, p. 144; Eng. trans. in *WTW*, p. 124; "L'Union créatrice" (1917), in *ET*, pp. 179–180; Eng. trans. in *WTW*, pp. 157–158; *GP*, p. 206; Eng. trans. in *MM*, p. 160; *GP*, pp. 210–211; Eng. trans. in *MM*, p. 163.

2. *"Note sur quelques représentations historiques possibles du péché originel" (1922), p. 7. Cf. "La Lutte contre la multitude" (1917), in *ET*, p. 123; Eng. trans. in *WTW*, p. 104.

3. "L'Esprit de la terre" (1931), *Oeuvres*, VI, p. 41. The discussion which begins at this point on the evolution of love and of the sexual sense incorporates some material previously published under the title of "Teilhard de Chardin's Vision of Love," *Thought*, XLII (1967), pp. 519–542.

4. "L'Eternel féminin" (1918), in *ET*, p. 253; Eng. trans. in *WTW*, p. 192.

5. *Ibid.*, p. 254; Eng. trans. in *WTW*, p. 193.

6. "La Centrologie" (1944), *Oeuvres*, VII, p. 125. Such an analogical use of the term "love" in relation to each stage of evolution is defended from a scientific point of view by the neurophysiologist Paul Chauchard, *Man and Cosmos* (New York, 1965), pp. 110–112, and from a philosophical point of view by Pitirim Sorokin, *The Ways and Power of Love* (Boston, 1954), p. 6.

7. "L'Eternel féminin" (1918), in *ET*, p. 254; Eng. trans. in *WTW*, p. 193.

8. *PH*, pp. 293–294; Eng. trans. pp. 264–265.

9. On the notion of activation, see "Action et activation" (1945), *Oeuvres*, IX, pp. 221–233; "L'Activation de l'énergie humaine" (1953), *Oeuvres*, VII, pp. 409–416; "Les Singularités de l'espèce humain" (1954), *Oeuvres*, II, pp. 357–366; Eng. trans. in *AM*, pp. 260–268.

10. "L'Esprit de la terre" (1931), *Oeuvres*. VI, p. 41. Cf. "Esquisse d'un univers personnel" (1936), *Oeuvres*, VI, pp. 91–96; "Le Phénomène spirituel" (1937), *Oeuvres*, VI, p. 133; "L'Energie humaine" (1937), *Oeuvres*, VI, pp. 161–162. For a somewhat more extensive discussion of Teilhard's thinking on sex than that provided here, see Emile Rideau, "La Sexualité selon le Père Teilhard de Chardin," *La Nouvelle Revue Théologique*, 90 (1968), pp. 173–190.

11. "Esquisse d'un universe personnel" (1936), *Oeuvres*, VI, p. 94. Cf. "L'Eternel féminin" (1918), in *ET*, p. 256; Eng. trans. in *WTW*, p. 195.

12. "L'Esprit de la terre" (1931), *Oeuvres*, VI, p. 42. Cf. "Le Phénomène humain (1930), *Oeuvres*, III, p. 242; Eng. trans. in *VP*, p. 173; "Esquisse d'un univers personnel" (1936), *Oeuvres*, VI, p. 93.

13. *LV*, p. 97; Eng. trans. in *LT*, p. 133.

14. Letter of October 30, 1936, in *Letters To Two Friends 1926–1952* (New York, 1968), p. 91.

15. *PH*, pp. 265–266; Eng. trans. pp. 239–240. Cf. *LV*, p. 97; Eng. trans. in *LT*, pp. 132–133; "La Montée de l'autre" (1942), *Oeuvres*, VII, pp. 69–70; "Un Grand Evénement qui se dessine: la planétisation humaine" (1945), *Oeuvres*, V, pp. 162–163; Eng. trans. in *FM*, pp. 127–128; "Note-Mémento sur la structure biologique de l'humanité" (1948), *Oeuvres*, IX, p. 269; *"Comment je vois" (1948), p. 11; *PN*, p. 140; Eng. trans., p. 97; "Réflexions sur la compression humaine" (1953), *Oeuvres*, VII, p. 359.

16. "Réflexions sur la compression humaine" (1953), *Oeuvres*, VII, p. 361. Cf. "Le Sens de la terre" (1931), *Oeuvres*, VI, p. 52; *PH*, pp. 318–319; Eng. trans. pp. 286–287; "Esquisse d'une dialectique de l'esprit" (1946), *Oeuvres*, VII, p. 151; "La Formation de la noosphère" (1947), *Oeuvres*, V, p. 227; Eng. trans. in *FM*, p. 179; *"Trois choses que je vois" (1948), p. 2; *"Comment je vois" (1948), pp. 11, n. 13, 12; "Les Singularités de l'espèce humain" (1954), *Oeuvres*, II, pp. 319–321, 366, n. 1; Eng. trans. in *AM*, pp. 229–230, 268, n. 1.

17. Cf. "L'Atomisme de l'esprit" (1941), *Oeuvres*, VII pp. 50–51; "La Centrologie" (1944), *Oeuvres*, VII, pp. 133–134; *PN*, p. 164, n. 1; Eng. trans. p. 144, n. 1; *"Le Phénomène chrétien" (1950), p. 5, n. 1; "La Structure phylétique du groupe humain" (1951), *Oeuvres*, II, p. 233, n. 1; Eng. trans. in *AM*, p. 170, n. 2; "Du Cosmos à la cosmogénèse" (1951), *Oeuvres*, VII, p. 273; "La Convergence de l'univers" (1951), *Oeuvres*, VII, p. 303; Cf. also the two letters cited by Henri de Lubac, *La Prière du Père Teilhard de Chardin* (Paris, 1964), pp. 53–54; Eng. trans., *Teilhard de Chardin: The Man and His Meaning* (New York, 1967), pp. 47–48.

18. *"Chute, rédemption et géocentrie" (1920), p. 2; "L'Esprit de la terre" (1931), *Oeuvres*, VI, p. 31; "Agitation ou Genèse?" (1947), *Oeuvres*, V, p. 277; Eng. trans. in *FM*, p. 216; *"Comment je vois" (1948), p. 4; *PN*, p. 50; Eng. trans. p. 35; "Qu'est-ce que la vie?" (1950), *Oeuvres*. IX, p. 275; "Du Pré-humain à l'ultra-humain" (1950), *Oeuvres*, V, p. 379; Eng. trans. in *FM*, p. 290. When Teilhard speaks of the cosmic function of Christ, he consistently argues in favor of the existence of numerous noospheres over all of which Christ would be Lord. See on this point: de Solages, pp. 204–207. However, the probable existence of a polynoospheric cosmos does not

necessarily entail the eventual linking up of the noospheres in history, and Teilhard generally did not consider such an eventuality as very likely, as we have seen.

19. "Du Pré-humain à l'ultra-humain" (1950), *Oeuvres*, V, p. 382; Eng. trans. in *FM*, p. 293; "Le Rebondissement humain de l'évolution et ses conséquences" (1947), *Oeuvres*, V, pp. 258–259; Eng. trans. in *FM*, p. 201; "Note Mémento sur la structure biologique de l'humanité" (1948), *Oeuvres*, IX, pp. 267–268. Teilhard argues in favor of the inventive factor being present in the pre-human stages of evolution in "Evolution zoologique et invention" (1947), *Oeuvres*, III, p. 330; Eng. trans. in *VP*, p. 235.

20. "Du Cosmos à la cosmogénèse" (1951), *Oeuvres*, VII, p. 273.

21. "Transformation et prolongements" (1951), *Oeuvres*, VII, p. 318. Cf. "Note sur la réalité actuelle et la signification évolutive d'une orthogénèse humaine" (1951), *Oeuvres*, III, p. 360; Eng. trans. in *VP*, p. 254; "Un Problème majeur pour l'anthropologie" (1951), *Oeuvres*, VII, p. 330.

22. This expression occurs in: "La Structure phylétique du groupe humain" (1951), *Oeuvres*, II, p. 225; Eng. trans. in *AM*. p. 163; "Du Cosmos à la cosmogénèse" (1951), *Oeuvres*, VII, p. 273; "Réflexions sur la probabilité scientifique" (1951), *Oeuvres*, VII, p. 287; "Transformation et prolongements en l'homme du méchanisme de l'évolution" (1951), *Oeuvres*, VII, p. 323; "Note sur la réalité actuelle et la signification évolutive d'une orthogénèse humaine" (1951), *Oeuvres*, III, p. 360; Eng. trans. in *VP*, p. 254; "Un Problème majeur pour l'anthropologie" (1951), *Oeuvres*, VII, p. 332; "L'Etoffe de l'univers" (1953), *Oeuvres*, VII, p. 405; *"Contingence de l'univers et goût humain de survivre" (1953), p. 1; "Les Singularités de l'espèce humain" (1954), *Oeuvres*, II, p. 349; Eng. trans. in *AM*, p. 253.

23. Teilhard had a certain fondness for repeating this text of Julian Huxley's: *PH*, p. 244; Eng. trans. p. 221; "La Place de l'homme dans l'univers" (1942), *Oeuvres*, III, p. 320; Eng. trans. in *VP*, p. 228; "Place de la technique dans une biologie générale de l'humanité" (1947), *Oeuvres*, VII, p. 168; "Evolution zoologique et invention" (1947), *Oeuvres*, III, p. 330; Eng. trans. in *VP*, p. 234; "Le Goût de vivre" (1950), *Oeuvres*, VII, p. 245; "Transformation et prolongements en l'homme du méchanisme de l'évolution" (1951), *Oeuvres*, VII, p. 322. A very similar expression, without any reference to Huxley, is used by Teilhard in "L'Esprit de la terre" (1931), *Oeuvres*, VI, p. 36.

24. *"Comment je vois" (1948), p. 10.

25. "La Formation de la noosphère" (1947), *Oeuvres*, V, pp. 223–224; Eng. trans. in *FM*, pp. 176–177. Cf. "Place de la technique dans une biologie générale de l'humanité" (1947), *Oeuvres*, VII. p. 167.

26. "Le Rebondissement humain de l'évolution" (1947), *Oeuvres*, V, pp. 254–255; Eng. trans. in *FM*, p. 197. Cf. "La Structure phylétique du groupe humain" (1951), *Oeuvres*, II, pp. 217–219; Eng. trans. in *AM*, pp. 157–159.

27. *PN*, pp. 159–160; Eng. trans., p. 111.

28. "Super-humanité, super-Christ, super-charité" (1943), *Oeuvres*, IX, pp. 202–205; "La Centrologie" (1944), *Oeuvres*, VII, p. 121; "Esquisse d'une dialectique de l'esprit" (1946). *Oeuvres*, VII, p. 150; "La Formation de la noosphère" (1947), *Oeuvres*, V, pp. 213–216; Eng. trans. in *FM*, pp. 166–169; "Place de la technique dans une biologie générale de l'humanité" (1947), *Oeuvres*, VII, p. 165; "La Structure phylétique du groupe humain"

(1951), *Oeuvres*, II, p. 224; Eng. trans. in *AM*, p. 163. Various qualifications of the accuracy of this analogy as applied to socialization are made in these texts.

29. Cf., for example, *PH*, pp. 158–159; Eng. trans. pp. 145–146; *PN*, pp. 67–70; Eng. trans. pp. 47–49.

30. Cf. n. 19.

31. *PH*, p. 265; Eng. trans. p. 239.

32. *PH*, pp. 271; Eng. trans. p. 244.

33. "L'Atomisme de l'esprit" (1941), *Oeuvres*, VII, p. 54. Cf. "Les Directions et les conditions de l'avenir" (1948), *Oeuvres*, V, p. 302; Eng. trans. in *FM*, p. 235; *PN*, p. 164; Eng. trans. p. 114. *"Le Coeur de la matière" (1950), p. 27.

34. "Mon Univers" (1924), *Oeuvres*, IX. p. 68.

35. "L'Avenir de l'homme vu par un paléontologiste" (1941), *Oeuvres*, V, p. 93–94; Eng. trans. in *FM*, pp. 69–70. Cf. *PH*, p. 270; Eng. trans. pp. 243–244.

36. *Ibid.*, p. 96; Eng. trans. in *FM*, p. 72.

37. "La Vie cosmique" (1916), in *ET*, p. 56; Eng. trans. in *WTW*, p. 67.

38. "Mon Univers" (1924), *Oeuvres*. IX, p. 110; "L'Hominisation" (1925), *Oeuvres*, III, pp. 106–107; Eng. trans. in *VP*, p. 75. Cf. "La Foi en l'homme" (1947), *Oeuvres*, V, p. 238; Eng. trans. in *FM*, p. 188; *PN*, p. 172; Eng. trans. p. 120; "L'Evolution de la responsabilité dans le monde" (1951), *Oeuvres*, VII, p. 218.

Chapter V

1. *PH*, pp. 295–296; Eng. trans., p. 266. Cf. "L'Energie humaine" (1937), *Oeuvres*, VI, pp. 156, 186–191; "La Montée de l'autre" (1942). *Oeuvres*, VII, pp. 78–79.

2. *PH*, p. 296; Eng. trans., pp. 266–267.

3. *PH*, pp. 297–298; Eng. trans., pp. 267–268.

4. Cf. de Lubac, pp. 249–250; Eng. trans., pp. 173–174, and de Solages, pp. 175–203, who gives a broader and fuller picture of Teilhard's use of the term "Omega" than does de Lubac.

5. "Sur l'existence probable, en avant de nous. d'un 'ultra-humain' " (1950), *Oeuvres*, V, p. 362; Eng. trans. in *FM*, p. 278.

6. "Comment concevoir et espérer que se réalise sur terre l'unanimisation humaine?" (1950), *Oeuvres*, V, p. 373; Eng. trans. in *FM*, p. 286.

7. *LV*, p. 176; Eng. trans. in *LT*, p. 202. Cf. "Mon Univers" (1924), *Oeuvres*, IX, pp. 70–71.

8. See, for example, the whole of "Barrière de la mort et co-réflexion" (1955), *Oeuvres*, VII, pp. 419–429.

9. On the attributes of Omega as transcendent, personal Center see de Solages, pp. 185–186.

10. On the Teilhardian "proofs" for the existence of God, see de Solages, pp. 240–252 and the same author's "Les Preuves teilhardiennes de Dieu," *L'Homme devant Dieu. Mélanges offerts à Henri de Lubac* (Paris, 1964), pp. 125–132.

11. * "Le Dieu de l'évolution" (1953), p. 5.

12. *Ibid.*, pp. 5–6.

13. Cf. Mooney, pp. 87–103.

14. "Oecuménisme" (1946), *Oeuvres*, IX, pp. 253–254.
15. *PH*, pp. 299–300; Eng. trans., p. 269.
16. *PH*, pp. 327–328; Eng. trans., pp. 293–294.
17. *PH*, pp. 324–325; Eng. trans., pp. 291–292. Cf. *"Comment je vois" (1948), p. 15; *"Introduction à la vie chrétienne" (1944), p. 6; "Esquisse d'une dialectique de l'esprit" (1946), *Oeuvres*, VII, pp. 150–155; * "Le Coeur de la matière" (1950), p. 20.
18. *"Comment je crois" (1934), p. 18.
19. It is necessary to observe at this point that Teilhard does not have in mind the virtue of supernatural faith here. Rather, he is speaking of faith in the sense in which he defined it in the Introduction to this same essay: "On the purely psychological plain where these pages intend to remain, I mean by 'faith' any commitment of our intelligence to a general perspective of the universe." A little further on, he says: "To believe is to achieve an intellectual synthesis." Obviously faith in this sense is simply a deeply held conviction arrived at by rational means.
20. *"Comment je crois" (1934), pp. 18–19.
21. For other texts in which Teilhard carries out a similar if not always identical type of critique, see: "Le Christianisme dans le monde" (1933), *Oeuvres*, IX, pp. 137–145; "Le Phénomène spirituel" (1937), *Oeuvres*, VI, pp. 135–136; *"Le Phénomène chrétien" (1950); "Réflexions sur deux formes inverses de l'esprit" (1950), *Oeuvres*. VII, pp. 233–235; *"Le Christique" (1955), pp. 10–11.
22. *"Comment je crois" (1934), pp. 21–22.
23. *Ibid.*, p. 22.
24. *Ibid.*, p. 22.
25. *PH*, p. 329; Eng. trans., p. 296.
26. *Ibid.*
27. "L'Energie humaine" (1937), *Oeuvres*, VI, pp. 193–194. Cf. *PH*, 332; Eng. trans., p. 198.
28. *PH*, pp. 331–332; Eng. trans.. pp. 297–298.
29. "L'Energie humaine" (1937), *Oeuvres*, VI, p. 192.
30. Cf. "Les Unités humaines naturelles" (1939), *Oeuvres*, III, pp. 289–290; Eng. trans. in *VP*, pp. 205–206; "La Place de l'homme dans l'univers" (1942), *Oeuvres*, III, p. 318; Eng. trans. in *VP*, p. 227; "Super-humanité, super-Christ, super-charité" (1943), *Oeuvres*, IX. pp. 216–218; "La Formation de la noosphère" (1947). *Oeuvres*, V, p. 229; Eng. trans. in *FM*, p. 182; "L'Energie d'évolution" (1953), *Oeuvres*, VII, p. 384, n. 2; *"Le Christique" (1955), p. 12.
31. *"Le Sens humain" (1929), p. 12. Cf. *"Christologie et évolution" (1933), p. 13; "Super-humanité, super-Christ, super-charité" (1943), *Oeuvres*, IX, pp. 212–213; *"Christianisme et évolution" (1945), p. 9; *"Ce que le monde attend en ce moment de l'Eglise" (1952), p. 4.
32. "L'Energie humaine" (1937), *Oeuvres*, VI, p. 192.

Chapter VI

1. See on this point, de Solages, pp. 72, 238, 268, n. 12; John L. Russell, S.J., "The Principle of Finality in the Philosophy of Aristotle and Teilhard de Chardin," *The Heythrop Journal*, III (October, 1962), pp. 347–357, IV (January, 1963), pp. 32–41.

2. This line unmistakably echoes Genesis 2, 18.
3. "La Lutte contre la multitude" (1917), in *ET*, pp. 115–116; Eng. trans. in *WTW*, p. 97. Cf. "L'Union créatrice" (1917), in *ET*, p. 180; Eng. trans. in *WTW*, p. 158; "Forma Christi" (1918), in *ET*, p. 338; Eng. trans. in *WTW*, p. 252.
4. "Mon Univers" (1924), *Oeuvres*, IX, p. 95, n. 1.
5. "Forma Christi" (1918), in *ET*, p. 338; Eng. trans. in *WTW*, p. 252.
6. "La Lutte contre la multitude" (1917), in *ET*, p. 124; Eng. trans. in *WTW*, p. 105. This text echoes John 11, 51–52. Cf. John 10, 1–18.
7. "Note sur le progrès" (1920), *Oeuvres*, V, pp. 34–35; Eng. trans. in *FM*, pp. 22–23. Cf. "La Lutte contre la multitude" (1917), in *ET*, p. 125; Eng. trans. in *WTW*, pp. 106–107. After 1920, this biblically based image of Christ as the universal Shepherd apparently disappears from Teilhard's writings, probably because it is insufficiently organic and hence does not satisfy the demands of Teilhard's understanding of the function of the cosmic Christ.
8. *GP*, p. 76; Eng. trans. in *MM*, p. 62.
9. "Le Prêtre" (1918), in *ET*, p. 299; Eng. trans. in *WTW*, p. 220.
10. "L'Elément universel" (1919), in *ET*, p. 410; Eng. trans. in *WTW*, p. 299. Cf. *"Note sur les modes de l'action divine dans l'univers" (1920), p. 3; "Science et Christ ou Analyse et Synthèse" (1921), *Oeuvres*, IX, p. 61; "La Messe sur le monde" (1923), in *HU*, p. 24; Eng. trans., p. 25; *"Comment je crois" (1934), p. 24; *"Christianisme et évolution" (1945), p. 6.
11. "Mon Univers" (1918), in *ET*, p. 274; "Forma Christi" (1918), in *ET*, p. 338; Eng. trans. in *WTW*, p. 252; "Note sur le Christ-Universel" (1920), *Oeuvres*, IX, p. 39, Cf. "Note sur le progrès" (1920), *Oeuvres*, V, p. 36; Eng. trans. in *FM*, p. 23; "Comment se pose aujourd'hui la question du transformisme" (1921), *Oeuvres*, III, p. 37; Eng. trans. in *VP*, p. 23; *"Panthéisme et Christianisme" (1923), pp. 10–11; "Mon Univers" (1924), *Oeuvres*, IX, pp. 83–84, 85–88; *MD*, pp. 42–44; Eng. trans., pp. 57–58; *"Christologie et évolution" (1933), p. 10; *"Comment je crois" (1934), pp. 22–25; "Esquisse d'un univers personnel" (1936), *Oeuvres*, VI, p. 113; "Sauvons l'humanité" (1936), *Oeuvres*, IX, p. 191; *PH*, pp. 326–328; Eng. trans., pp. 293–294; "Super-humanité, super-Christ, super-charité" (1943), *Oeuvres*, IX, pp. 210–212; "Catholicisme et science" (1946), *Oeuvres*, IX, pp. 239–240; *"Réflexions sur le péché originel" (1947), p. 3; *"Le Christique" (1955), p. 8.
12. On this point see Mooney, p. 85.
13. "Forma Christi" (1918), in *ET*, p. 335; Eng. trans. in *WTW*, p. 250.
14. *Ibid.*, pp. 335–336; Eng. trans. in *WTW*, pp. 250–251.
15. *Ibid.*, p. 339; Eng. trans. in *WTW*, pp. 253–254.
16. *Ibid.*, pp. 350–351; Eng. trans. in *WTW*, p. 266. Cf. "L'Elément universel" (1919), in *ET*, p. 408; Eng. trans. in *WTW*, pp. 297–298; "Mon Univers" (1924), *Oeuvres*, IX, pp. 85, 93, 104; *"Christologie et évolution" (1933), p. 10.
17. *"Le Dieu de l'évolution" (1953), p. 3. Cf. "Du Cosmos à la cosmogénèse" (1951), *Oeuvres*, VII, pp. 270–271; *"Le Phénomène chrétien" (1950), p. 3; *"Comment je vois" (1948), pp. 18–19; "Esquisse d'une dialectique de l'esprit" (1946), *Oeuvres*, VII, p. 158. For the development of this theme during the First World War period see "L'Union créatrice" (1917), in *ET*, p. 186 and n. 10; Eng. trans. in *WTW*, p. 164; Journal entries of October 1, 1918, and October 3, 1918, cited in de Solages, p. 318.

18. "Forma Christi" (1918), in *ET*, p. 350, n. 13; Eng. trans. in *WTW*, p. 265. De Solages, pp. 193–194, 248–249, argues that efficient causality does play a role in Teilhard's thought, thus assuring that his Omega functions also as an Alpha. Cf. "L'Elément universel" (1919), in *ET*, pp. 406–407; Eng. trans. in *WTW*, pp. 295–296.

19. Cf. the discussion in Smulders, pp. 68–70; Eng. trans., pp. 57–59, on Teilhard's attempt to rethink the imagery of creation in terms of final and formal causality.

20. The first clear instance of the formula occurs in *"Comment je crois" (1934), p. 16, n. 1: "Genuine union (that is spiritual or synthetic union) differentiates the elements which it brings together." In the autumn of the following year, Teilhard writes to Lucile Swan: "My present topic is more and more *L'Union différencie*. There is a full metaphysics, ethic, and mystic, contained in those three words." Lucile Swan, "Memories and Letters," *Teilhard de Chardin: Pilgrim of the Future*, ed. Neville Braybrooke (New York, 1964), p. 43. From this point on, occurrences of the formula are frequent. Further references may be found in Mooney, pp. 225, n. 22 and 256, n. 81.

21. Cf. "La Vie cosmique" (1916), in *ET*, pp. 37–38; Eng. trans. in *WTW*, pp. 47–48; "La Lutte contre la multitude" (1917), in *ET*, p. 131; Eng. trans. in *WTW*, p. 113; "L'Union créatrice" (1917), in *ET*, p. 189, n. 11; Eng. trans. in *WTW*, p. 167; Journal entry of March 8, 1918, cited in de Solages, p. 197, n. 103; "Le Prêtre" (1918), in *ET*, p. 292; Eng. trans. in *WTW*, p. 213; Journal entry of October 3, 1918, cited in de Solages, p. 191, n. 88; "Forma Christi" (1918), in *ET*, p. 351; Eng. trans. in *WTW*, p. 266; "Note sur l'élément universel du monde" (1918), in *ET*, p. 362; Eng. trans. in *WTW*, p. 275; Journal entry of January 1, 1919, cited in de Solages, p. 268, n. 1; "L'Elément universel" (1919), in *ET*, p. 410; Eng. trans. in *WTW*, p. 299; Journal entry of February 4, 1920, cited in de Solages, p. 191, n. 88; Journal entry of February 10, 1920, cited in de Solages, p. 271, n. 16; *"Panthéisme et christianisme" (1923), p. 10; "La Messe sur le monde" (1923), in *HU*, p. 26; Eng. trans. pp. 26–27; "Mon Univers" (1924), *Oeuvres*, IX, p. 74; *MD*, pp. 137, 139, 142; *Eng. trans.*, pp. 114, 116, 118; "L'Esprit de la terre" (1931), *Oeuvres*, VI, p. 52; *"La Route de l'Ouest" (1932), p. 16.

22. Cf. "La Vie cosmique" (1916), in *ET*, p. 41; Eng. trans. in *WTW*, p. 51; "L'Union créatrice" (1917), in *ET*, p. 193; Eng. trans. in *WTW*, p. 171; "Note sur le progrès" (1920), *Oeuvres*, V, p. 35; Eng. trans. in *FM*, p. 23. *"Panthéisme et christianisme" (1923), p. 11.

23. "L'Union créatrice" (1917), in *ET*, p. 196; Eng. trans. in *WTW*, p. 174. Writing on November 10, 1917 (the same month in which "L'Union créatrice" was composed), in his Journal, Teilhard remarks: "The full significance of the theory of creative union is to be found in the doctrine of the Body of Christ." Cited in de Solages, p. 202, n. 115. Cf. "Mon Univers" (1918), in *ET*, p. 277.

24. "Mon Univers" (1924), *Oeuvres*, IX, pp. 81–82. Cf. de Lubac, p. 118; Eng. trans., p. 87.

25. On the relationship between the mystical and cosmic Bodies, see "La Vie cosmique" (1916), in *ET*, pp. 47–49; Eng. trans. in *WTW*, pp. 57–59; "L'Union créatrice" (1917), in *ET*, pp. 196–197; Eng. trans. in *WTW*, p. 175; "La Lutte contre la multitude" (1917), in *ET*, p. 128; Eng. trans.

in *WTW*, p. 110; "L'Elément universel" (1919), in *ET*, p. 408; Eng. trans. in *WTW*, p. 297.

26. "L'Union créatrice" (1917), in *ET*, p. 196; Eng. trans. in *WTW*, p. 174.

27. *"Christianisme et évolution" (1949), p. 8. Cf. *"Réflexions sur le péché originel" (1947), p. 7; *"Comment je vois" (1948), pp. 17, n. 26, 18–19, 20–21; *"Le Coeur de la matière" (1950), p. 30.

28. *MD*, p. 149; Eng. trans., p. 122.

29. Mooney, p. 177.

30. "Esquisse d'une dialectique de l'esprit" (1946), *Oeuvres*, VII, p. 156.

31. Mooney, pp. 174–175. Cf. the comments by Smulders, pp. 95–96; Eng. trans., pp. 82–83. Smulders allows for the creation introducing "change" in God, but he insists that this is so only because God freely allows it to by freely creating. He suspects Teilhard of making such "change" compulsive because God "needs" to create.

32. "L'Ame du monde" (1918), in *ET*, p. 231; Eng. trans. in *WTW*, pp. 189–190.

33. *"Contingence de l'univers et goût humain de survivre" (1953), p. 4.

34. Cited in de Solages, p. 336.

35. Cf. "La Vie cosmique" (1916), in *ET*, pp. 57–58; Eng. trans. in *WTW*, pp. 68–69; "La Maîtrise du monde et le règne de Dieu" (1916), in *ET*, pp. 83–84; Eng. trans. in *WTW*, p. 91; "Le Christ dans la matière" (1916), in *ET*, pp. 100–101; Eng. trans. in *HU*, p. 49; "La Lutte contre la multitude" (1917), in *ET*, p. 132; Eng. trans. in *WTW*, p. 114; *GP*, p. 230; Eng. trans. in *MM*, p. 178; "L'Union créatrice" (1917), in *ET*, p. 195; Eng. trans. in *WTW*, p. 173; "L'Ame du monde" (1918), in *ET*, pp. 231–232; Eng. trans. in *WTW*, p. 190; "Le Prêtre" (1918), in *ET*, p. 298; Eng. trans. in *WTW*, p. 218; "Forma Christi" (1918), in *ET*, pp. 349–350, 353; Eng. trans. in *WTW*, pp. 265, 269; "Terre promise" (1919), in *ET*, p. 395; Eng. trans. in *WTW*, pp. 286–287; "Les Noms de la matière" (1919), in *ET*, pp. 426–427, 429; "Note sur le progrès" (1920), *Oeuvres*, V, p. 31; Eng. trans. in *FM*, p. 19; Journal entry of November 1, 1921, cited in de Solages, p. 350, n. 38; *"Panthéisme et christianisme" (1923), p. 12; "La Messe sur le monde" (1923), p. 34; Eng. trans. in *HU*, pp. 34–35; "Mon Univers" (1924), *Oeuvres*, IX, pp. 113–114.

36. *MD*, p. 189; Eng. trans., pp. 147–148.

37. *MD*, pp. 191–192; Eng. trans., p. 149.

38. *"Introduction à la vie chrétienne" (1944), pp. 8–9.

39. Mooney, p. 124.

Chapter VII

1. Smulders, p. 213; Eng. trans. pp. 199–200.

2. *MD*, p. 139; Eng. trans. p. 116.

3. "La Vie cosmique" (1916), in *ET*, pp. 37, 39, 59; Eng. trans. in *WTW*, pp. 47, 49, 70.

4. "La Lutte contre la multitude" (1917), in *ET*, p. 129; Eng. trans. in *WTW*, p. 111.

5. "Le Milieu mystique" (1917), in *ET*, pp. 163–164; Eng. trans. in *WTW*, pp. 144–145.

6. "L'Union créatrice" (1917), in *ET*, p. 197; Eng. trans. in *WTW*, p. 175.

7. *MD*, p. 150; Eng. trans. p. 123. It is worth noting at this point that the term "*milieu*" in French "has no exact equivalent in English as it implies both centre and environment or setting" (cf. the English edition of *The Divine Milieu*, p. 9). In other words, the term "milieu" can refer either to a center or the circumambiance created by that center or both together. When the term is applied to Christ, it should be capitalized and understood as a title equivalent to the term "Center." We have, generally speaking, been using the term in the sense of an environment or circumambiance created by the omnipresence of Christ, and hence we have been considering it as being equivalent to the notion of the Body of Christ. Whether one chooses to think primarily of center or environment is merely a matter of emphasis, since the term necessarily includes both aspects simultaneously.

8. Teilhard returns to the notion of the divine milieu later in his career in *"Le Coeur de la matière" (1950), pp. 27–29; and *"Le Christique" (1955), pp. 9–10.

9. "Mon Univers" (1918), in *ET*, p. 275.

10. *Ibid.*, p. 275. This formula appears the same year in "Forma Christi" (1918), in *ET*, p. 344; Eng. trans. in *WTW*, p. 259, in a slightly altered form: *"Quidquid patimur, Christum patimur. Quidquid agimus, Christus agitur."* Whatever we undergo, we undergo Christ. Whatever we do is done to Christ.

11. "L'Energie humaine" (1937), *Oeuvres*, VI, p. 192. Cf. *MD*, p. 133; Eng. trans. p. 112.

12. "Mon Univers" (1924), *Oeuvres*, IX, pp. 94–95.

13. "Mon Univers" (1924), *Oeuvres*, IX, p. 73.

14. N. M. Wildiers, *Teilhard de Chardin* (Paris, 1960), pp. 9–10; Eng. trans., *An Introduction to Teilhard de Chardin* (New York, 1968), p. 26. Cf. de Solages, pp. 3–16.

15. Cf. *On the Boundary: An Autobiographical Sketch* (New York, 1966).

16. *"Comment je crois" (1934), p. 1. Cf. *"Christologie et évolution" (1933), p. 1.

17. "Le Prêtre" (1918). in *ET*, p. 287; Eng. trans. in *WTW*, p. 207. Cf. "Le Milieu mystique" (1917), in *ET*, pp. 164–165; Eng. trans. in *WTW*, p. 146.

18. Letter of March, 1916, to Victor Fontoynont, cited in de Lubac, p. 350; Eng. trans. p. 245. The following month Teilhard completed "La Vie cosmique" which is prefaced by the following text: "There is a communion with God and a communion with the earth and also a communion with God through the earth." In *ET*, p. 5; Eng. trans. in *WTW*, p. 14.

19. "La Messe sur le monde" (1923), *HU*, p. 19, Eng. trans. p. 20. Cf. "Le Prêtre" (1918). in *ET*, pp. 288–289; Eng. trans. in *WTW*, pp. 209–210; *"Le Christique" (1955), p. 9.

20. *LV*, p. 46; Eng. trans. in *LT*, p. 86.

21. Ernst Benz, *Evolution and Christian Hope* (Garden City, N.Y., 1966), pp. 224–225.

22. Cf. on this point, the copious citations in Henri de Lubac, *Catholicism* (New York, 1965), ch. III.

23. "La Lutte contre la multitude" (1917), in *ET*, p. 126; Eng. trans. in *WTW*, p. 108.

24. *The Confessions* (New York, 1942), translation by Frank J. Sheed. bk. X, ch. XXIX, p. 193.

25. Soren Kierkegaard, *Purity of Heart Is to Will One Thing* (New York, 1956).

26. This expression, taken from Luke 10, 42, is used a number of times by Teilhard. The expression usually, but not always, refers to Christ. Cf. de Lubac, pp. 40–41; Eng. trans. p. 32; *Blondel et Teilhard de Chardin* (Paris, 1965), p. 73, n. 22; Eng. trans. *Blondel-Teilhard Correspondence* (New York, 1967), pp. 84–85. In both these places de Lubac notes the influence of Maurice Blondel on Teilhard's use of the expression.

27. *MD*, pp. 165–168; Eng. trans., pp. 132–134; "Le Milieu mystique" (1917), in *ET*, pp. 153–154; Eng. trans. in *WTW*, pp. 134–135.

28. "La Lutte contre la multitude" (1917), in *ET*, pp. 126–127; Eng. trans. in *WTW*, pp. 108–109.

29. Cf. the treatment of this thematic in Robert Faricy, S.J., *Teilhard de Chardin's Theology of the Christian in the World* (New York, 1967), pp. 181–196.

30. "La Lutte contre la multitude" (1917), in *ET*, p. 120; Eng. trans. in *WTW*, p. 102.

31. de Lubac, p. 166; Eng. trans.. p. 119. This tradition has been treated by de Lubac himself with numerous citations in ch. I of his work *Catholicism*.

32. *MD*, p. 80, n. 1; Eng. trans., p. 80, n. 1.

33. "La Lutte contre la multitude" (1917), in *ET*, pp. 120–121; Eng. trans. in *WTW*, pp. 102–103.

34. Apart from "La Lutte contre la multitude," the longest treatment of the theme occurs in "L'Union créatrice" (1917), in *ET*, pp. 194–195; Eng. trans. in *WTW*, pp. 172–173. Briefer indications that the theme is still operative in Teilhard's thinking will be found in: "L'Ame du monde" (1918), in *ET*, p. 229; Eng. trans. in *WTW*, p. 187; "Le Prêtre" (1918), in *ET*, pp. 300–301; Eng. trans. in *WTW*, pp. 221–222; "La Foi qui opère" (1918), in *ET*, p. 329; Eng. trans. in *WTW*, p. 247; "Note pour servir à l'évangélisation des temps nouveaux" (1919), in *ET*, p. 378; "La Messe sur le monde" (1923), in *HU*, p. 36; Eng. trans., p. 36. In *The Divine Milieu*, Teilhard treats sensuality and egoism under the single topic of purity; *MD*, p. 166, Eng. trans., p. 133.

35. *"Le Coeur de la matière" (1950), pp. 7–8.

36. *GP*, pp. 73–74; Eng. trans. in *MM*, p. 60. Cf. *GP*, pp. 75–77; Eng. trans. in *MM*, pp. 61–63; "La Vie cosmique" (1916), in *ET*, pp. 19–23; Eng. trans. in *WTW*, pp. 28–32.

37. Letter of March 15, 1916, to Victor Fontoynont, cited in de Lubac. pp. 349–350; Eng. trans., p. 244; "La Vie cosmique" (1916), in *ET*, p. 19; Eng. trans. in *WTW*, p. 28; "Le Milieu mystique" (1917), in *ET*, p. 141; Eng. trans. in *WTW*, p. 121; *"Panthéisme et christianisme" (1923), p. 7.

38. "L'Elément universel" (1919), in *ET*, 403–409; Eng. trans. in *WTW*, pp. 292–298.

39. Teilhard frequently sees in Christianity the fulfillment rather than the negation of his own pantheistic aspirations and those of the contemporary world: Letter of March 15, 1916, to Victor Fontoynont, cited in de Lubac, p. 350; Eng. trans., p. 244; "La Vie cosmique" (1916), in *ET*, pp. 49–50; Eng. trans. in *WTW*, pp. 60–61; "Le Christ dans la matière" (1916), in *ET*, p. 105; Eng. trans. in *HU*, pp. 53–54; "L'Ame du monde" (1918), in *ET*, pp. 230–232; Eng. trans. in *WTW*, pp. 188–190; "Note sur l'élément universel du monde" (1918), in *ET*, pp. 361–362; Eng. trans. in *WTW*, pp. 274–275;

"Note pour servir à l'évangélisation des temps nouveaux" (1919), in *ET*, p. 372; *"Panthéisme et christianisme" (1923), p. 1; "La Messe sur le monde" (1923), in *HU*, pp. 25–26; Eng. trans., pp. 26–27; *"Comment je crois" (1934), p. 24; *"Quelques vues générales sur l'essence du christianisme" (1939), pp. 2–3; *"Introduction à la vie chrétienne" (1944), p. 13; "Réflexions sur deux formes inverses de l'esprit" (1950), *Oeuvres*, VII, pp. 233–235.

40. "La Lutte contre la multitude" (1917), in *ET*, p. 119; Eng. trans. in *WTW*, p. 101.

41. Cf. de Solages, pp. 4–5.

42. "L'Elément universel" (1919), in *ET*, p. 404; Eng. trans. in *WTW*, p. 293.

43. In *MD*, p. 26; Eng. trans., p. 47, Teilhard, echoing the Chalcedonian christological formula describing the two natures in Christ, writes: "Without mixture, without confusion, the true God, the Christian God, will, under your very gaze, invade the universe, our universe of today, the universe which so frightened you by its alarming size or its pagan beauty. He will penetrate it as a ray of light penetrates crystal; and, with the help of the great layers of creation, he will become for you universally perceptible and active— very near and very distant at one and the same time." This text indicates with perfect clarity that the Omega, Christ, the incarnate presence of God in the world, is both the immanent and transcendent Center of evolution, in whom nature and the supernatural are indeed synthesized, but without confusion or identification.

44. Cf. "Note sur l'élément universel du monde" (1918), in *ET*, pp. 359–362; Eng. trans. in *WTW*, pp. 272–276; "L'Elément universel" (1919), in *ET*, pp. 401–409; Eng. trans. in *WTW*, pp. 290–298; "Mon Univers" (1924), *Oeuvres*, IX, p. 87.

45. *"Panthéisme et christianisme" (1923), p. 1.

46. Cf. the observations of Henri de Lubac in this regard in *Blondel et Teilhard de Chardin*, p. 9; Eng. trans., *Blondel-Teilhard Correspondence*, p. 10; and the pertinent letters in *GP*, pp. 390, 393, 397–398; Eng. trans. in *MM*, pp. 298, 300, 303–304.

47. *"Panthéisme et christianisme" (1923), pp. 8–13.

48. *Ibid.*, p. 3.

49. *"La Route de l'Ouest" (1932), p. 1.

50. *Ibid.*, pp. 2–3.

51. *Ibid.*, pp. 12–18.

52. "Note pour servir à l'évangélisation des temps nouveaux" (1919), in *ET*, p. 380.

53. *"La Route de l'Ouest" (1932), p. 11.

54. *Ibid.*, p. 12.

55. *Ibid.*, p. 15.

56. *Ibid.*, p. 15.

57. Cf. on this point, Mooney, pp. 181–188, who also cites the appropriate texts.

58. "Réflexions sur deux formes inverses de l'esprit" (1950), *Oeuvres*, VII, p. 226.

59. *Ibid.*

60. "Action et activation" (1945), *Oeuvres*, IX, p. 230.

61. "Esquisse d'un univers personnel" (1936), *Oeuvres*. VI, p. 103. Cf. *PH*, pp. 291, 327, 344; Eng. trans., pp. 262, 294, 310.

62. *"Introduction à la vie chrétienne" (1944), p. 13. Cf. *"Quelques remarques 'pour y voir clair' sur l'essence du sentiment mystique" (1951), p. 1.

63. "Réflexions sur deux formes inverses de l'esprit" (1950), *Oeuvres*, VII, p. 231.

64. Letter of October, 1923, in *LV*, p. 61; Eng. trans. in *LT*, p. 101.

65. Letter of September 8, 1935, in *LV*, p. 186; Eng. trans. in *LT*, p. 207.

66. This text is used by Teilhard in *"Panthéisme et christianisme" (1923), p. 13; "Mon Univers" (1924), *Oeuvres*, IX, p. 114; *MD*, p. 139; Eng. trans., p. 116; *"La Route de l'Ouest (1932), p. 15; *PH*, p. 327; Eng. trans., p. 294; *"Introduction à la vie chrétienne" (1944), pp. 1, 13; "Réflexions sur deux formes inverses de l'esprit" (1950), *Oeuvres*, VII, p. 232; *"Quelques remarques 'pour y voir clair' sur l'essence du sentiment mystique" (1951), p. 1; Journal entry of April 7, 1955, cited in *Oeuvres*, V, pp. 404–405; Eng. trans. in *FM*, p. 309.

67. "Mon Univers" (1924), *Oeuvres*, IX, p. 94.

68. *Ibid.*, p. 114.

Concluding Summary

1. "L'Union créatrice" (1917), in *ET*, p. 178; Eng. trans. in *WTW*, p. 156.

2. Cf. "Mon Univers" (1918), in *ET*, p. 277.

3. Cf. "L'Esprit de la terre" (1931), *Oeuvres*, VI, p. 30; *PH*, p. 154; Eng. trans., p. 142.

4. *PH*, p. 25; Eng. trans., p. 31.

5. "Mon Univers" (1924). *Oeuvres*, IX, p. 94.

Acknowledgements

Acknowledgement and grateful appreciation are due to Harper & Row for permission to use copyrighted material from the following books by Teilhard de Chardin: *The Phenomenon of Man*, copyright © 1959 by Wm. Collins Sons & Co., London, and Harper & Row, Publishers, Incorporated, New York (revised edition, 1965); *The Divine Milieu*, copyright © 1960 by Wm. Collins Sons & Co., London, and Harper & Row, Publishers, Incorporated, New York; *The Future of Man*, copyright © 1964 by Wm. Collins Sons & Co., London, and Harper & Row, Publishers, Incorporated, New York.

The author also wishes to express his appreciation to *Thought* for permission to use excerpts of a previously published article entitled "Teilhard de Chardin's Vision of Love" which appeared in their Winter 1967 issue. This article was later reprinted in *Dimensions of the Future*, edited by Marvin Kessler and Bernard Brown and published by Corpus Books in 1968. Corpus Books has also generously granted permission for the use of this excerpted material.

Permission has also been kindly granted by Holt, Rinehart, and Winston to quote from the *Complete Poems of Robert Frost*, copyright © 1949 by Holt, Rinehart, and Winston, Inc.

The author wishes, in addition, to acknowledge with appreciation the use of material from Volume Six of the *Oeuvres* of Pierre Teilhard de Chardin, copyright © 1962 by Editions du Seuil, Paris, from Volume Seven of the *Oeuvres*, copyright © 1963 by Editions du Seuil, Paris, and from Volume Nine of the *Oeuvres*, copyright © 1965 by Editions du Seuil, Paris. Appreciative acknowledgement is also in order for the use of material from *Ecrits du Temps de la Guerre*, copyright © 1965 by Editions Bernard Grasset. All the texts quoted from these French volumes have, of course, been rendered directly into English by the author himself. Furthermore, a number of other texts were translated by the author directly from the French, even where English translations existed at the time of writing.